SO-EBR-328

The
EFFIE LEE
MORRIS

★ HISTORICAL AND RESEARCH COLLECTION ★
OF CHILDREN'S LITERATURE

SAN FRANCISCO PUBLIC LIBRARY

'71 -21

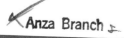

I HAVE A DREAM *is a book about the Negro Civil Rights Movement. Taking its title from Martin Luther King's stirring Washington March Speech, the book focuses on the Activist Movement through the dreams and goals of the Negro leaders.*

I Have a Dream

I Have a Dream

by *Emma Gelders Sterne*

illustrated by *Tracy Sugarman*

ALFRED A. KNOPF · NEW YORK

The author gratefully acknowledges permission to reprint the following: "Merry-go-round" by Langston Hughes from SHAKESPEARE IN HARLEM, Alfred A. Knopf, 1942; from PERSONALS by Arna Bontemps, Paul Breman (limited edition), London 1963; from MY LORD, WHAT A MORNING by Marian Anderson, Viking Press, Inc.; "Let America Be America Again" by Langston Hughes from THE POETRY OF THE NEGRO, edited by Langston Hughes and Arna Bontemps, published by Doubleday and Co., reprinted by permission from the author; "Heritage" (first stanza) by Countee Cullen. Copyright 1925 by Harper & Brothers, renewed 1953 by Ida M. Cullen, reprinted by the permission of Harper & Row Publishers; from A STAR TO STEER BY by Hugh Mulzac, International Publishers Co. Inc.; from WHEN THE WORD IS GIVEN by Louis Lomax, Harper & Row, Publishers; from "Montgomery, Alabama; Money, Mississippi, And Other Places" by Eve Merriam, Cameron Associates, 1956; from WHY WE CAN'T WAIT by Martin Luther King, Jr., Harper & Row, Publishers; from LONG SHADOW OF LITTLE ROCK by Daisy Bates, David McKay Company, Inc.; "Street Scene—1946" by Kenneth Porter, "Common Ground," summer 1947 issue; James Farmer as quoted in James Peck's FREEDOM RIDE, Simon And Schuster, Inc.; "Vulcan and Mars Over Birmingham" by John Beecher from REPORT TO THE STOCKHOLDERS AND OTHER POEMS, Monthly Review Press, 1962; excerpt from "Poem" by Bob Dylan, from the jacket cover of "Another Side of Bob Dylan" (Columbia CL2193), reprinted by permission of Albert B. Grossman Management, Inc.

L.C. Catalog card number: 65–12076

THIS IS A BORZOI BOOK, PUBLISHED BY ALFRED A. KNOPF, INC.

For Ella Baker,
WHOSE OWN DREAM IS ENCOMPASSED IN THE WORK
OF THE YOUNG PEOPLE SHE HAS INSPIRED

A Note from the Author

The title of this book, *I Have A Dream*, is taken from Dr. Martin Luther King's historic speech in Washington on August 28, 1963. But the words have a special significance for me. For many years, I have been torn between the desire to continue writing for young people and an intense preoccupation with the events surrounding the struggle of the Negro people to step into their rightful place as American citizens. To put down the story of this struggle in terms which I hope will appeal to the boys and girls standing on the threshold of the struggle is, for me, a dream come true.

The portraits I have drawn are, in no sense, definitive biographies, though I have gone to great pains to make them conform to the truth as I see it. The broad outlines are, of course, based on factual material, but I have "invented" scenes and dialogue deduced from a hint here, a word or phrase there, occasionally spoken in a different context.

Many of the people I have been privileged, over my long life, to know personally. Others have been friends of my friends for whose help and advice I am most grateful. Several have published their own memoirs, from which I have liberally drawn. I have also had inestimable assistance from librarians at San Jose State College and the San Jose Public Library; from the courageous workers in the Congress of Racial Equality (CORE) and the Student Non-Violent Coordinating Committee (SNCC); from Virginia Durr and Anne Braden. Also, I am in debt to more people than I can mention for assistance and encouragement in preparing this book, and particularly to my daughter, Barbara Lindsay, and to Virginie Fowler and Jane Yolen for their careful research and editing.

The full story will some day supplant these fragmentary biographical sketches. Each of the people, and many more who are barely mentioned, deserve full biographies. The story is not yet complete, nor will it be until skin color becomes so unimportant on the American scene—and the world scene—that the book itself is outdated and forgotten.

By a curious coincidence of history, the story begins and ends on the steps of the Memorial to Abraham Lincoln in Washington, D.C. Its real beginning, however, was in the long past; its real ending in the future. That future began in 1963, when 250,000 Americans, Negro and white, converged on the nation's capital to proclaim *Freedom Now*, and to hear their own innermost hopes voiced in the words of Martin Luther King: *I Have A Dream* . . . .

Emma Gelders Sterne
San Jose, California, 1965

Contents

Introduction

"A Century New for the Duty and the Deed"

To try to understand the young men and women and the children who are the chief actors in this story of today's Freedom Movement without knowing something of the history of Negro Americans for the last three hundred years is like trying to put together a jigsaw puzzle with half the pieces missing. Even if you have studied what is called American history in school—its government, its presidents, its wars, its often heroic progress—still the saga of the Negro American, essential to the whole picture, is probably foggy and unclear.

From the day kidnapped Africans were first landed on the North American mainland in 1526, through the years of servitude and developing slavery in the English colonies, through the American Revolution and the Civil War and two World Wars, what was really happening to Americans of African descent was hardly considered at all in a society controlled by European Americans. It made little difference to "white" America what "black" America thought or dreamed or willed. "This is a white man's country"—it was said aloud for many years and, traditionally, accepted for many more. And white men wrote the history books that were focused only upon Europe's contribution to the United States.

It was left largely to scholars in our time to search out the dramatic story of African Americans. Modern historians such as Carter G. Woodson, W. E. B. Du Bois, Herbert Aptheker, Arna Bontemps, J. A. Rogers, Kenneth M. Stampp, and others had to search old records, diaries, newspapers, and the petitions from Africans and African Americans (slave and free) to Congress. They had to fit the bits and pieces together. From the findings of archeologists, digging in the ruins of African cities buried for hundreds of years, and from manuscripts written on parchment during the Middle Ages, they reconstructed the story of the proud civilizations from which Negro Americans came.

They brought to light, at last, the fierce struggles for freedom in the years of American enslavement; gave meaning to the names of leaders such as Gabriel Prosser, Denmark Vesey, Nat Turner. They made it possible to read the eloquent pleas for equal citizenship, lying unread and ignored by Congress after Congress. They brought into daylight the story of the Underground Railroad by which, with unimagined heroism, over fifty thousand Negro Americans emancipated themselves before the Civil War and broke open the bonds of slavery. Painstakingly, they explored reports of the colleagues of the great Negro abolitionist, Frederick Douglass; of the two hundred thousand dark-skinned soldiers who fought in the Union armies for their countrymen's freedom; of the legislators and teachers in the brief years of Reconstruction. To unearth the actual facts, they had to dig almost as deep as the archeologists who searched out the ruins of cities in the African deserts and forests.

Most of the pioneering group were Negro Americans who had had a struggle of their own to prepare themselves in order to take a place in the ranks of historical scholars. There were, in the South, only three real institutions of higher learning which Negro students could attend—Howard University, founded by the United States Government after Emancipation, Fisk University, and Atlanta University. There were no public high schools at the close of the nineteenth century that would accept Negro students, and less than a dozen schools of high school level, all founded with the help of charitable and wealthy northerners. The gifts and grants for the education of Negro boys and girls had ceased to flow freely from the religious organizations to those separate, sectarian boarding schools teaching Latin and Greek and preparing students for entrance to first-rate colleges. Funds were going, instead, to so-called Industrial Schools like Tuskegee which offered limited book training and more emphasis on the making of a good servant or the best methods of growing cotton or sweet potatoes on land not their own.

White Southerners were grateful to the former slave, Booker T. Washington, for the kind of education he offered at Tuskegee and for teaching Negroes to be industrious and obedient and to "know their place." So they, too, gave money to schools that did not make scholars or rouse discontent and talk of rights under the Constitution.

This meant children growing up without knowledge of their own great history; children finding it hard to respect themselves because they were not respected; children hemmed in, wherever they lived, by a high wall called segregation or nicknamed, ruefully, Jim Crow after a comic minstrel show character—a parody figure.

In the South, as soon as a child could speak, he learned: "Don't do this, don't do that." "Use the back door when you have to go in the white folks' house." "Don't look a white person straight in the eye." "Sit in the back on a bus." "Say 'sir' or 'ma'am' every time you speak to them." The parents taught these things. They had to for their children's protection. Only "uppity" Negroes forgot to act inferior—and "uppity" Negroes sometimes got taken out by the Ku Klux Klan and were beaten or lynched and hung from a tree. Seven hundred and sixty-five innocent men and women lost their lives in this way from 1900 to 1910.

In the North, Jim Crow didn't walk by your side and in front of you and behind you every hour of every day. But the unwritten laws of a separate life were there. Only five *Northern* states permitted Negro Americans to vote until *after* the 14th Amendment was ratified in 1868.

The best colleges in the country were open to qualified Negroes; but parents could rarely save enough to afford to educate their children beyond the public high school. Most of the Negro Americans with higher education became teachers or ministers of the Gospel, some keeping alive the quest for freedom, but many preached acceptance of things-as-they-were on Booker T. Washington's terms. The number of students who did postgraduate work could be counted on the fingers of one hand, but among this group was John Hope of Atlanta University. It was he who, at the beginning of the twentieth century, brought New England-born William Edward Burghardt Du Bois South to teach in Atlanta. Du Bois had studied at Fisk in Nashville, Tennessee, and had earned his way through college each summer by teaching in country schools and "boarding around" with the farming families of his pupils. He was therefore acquainted with the conditions of the Negro people in the South. But he had also studied for five years at Harvard University and for two years in Germany and had published important books before coming to Atlanta—one on the suppression of the African slave trade and the other a survey on the conditions confronting the Philadelphia Negro, the first of the famous *Historical Studies* published by Harvard University.

The research for these books had given Du Bois a knowledge of the African background of the Negro American and the ruin American slavery had brought in past centuries to the ancient kingdoms on the African continent. During the Philadelphia research, he was made aware of the abandoned dreams of the Negro citizen of a Northern city. He had not been in Atlanta long before he began to write and publish in national literary magazines. In 1903, these brilliant essays on the life of Negro Americans were gathered in one volume—*The Souls of Black Folk.*

This book and its writer changed the history of the Negro people in the United States. Not all at once and not without setbacks, but never again after the publication of *The Souls of Black Folk* could a thinking, intelligent person—black or white—believe that "the world belongs to white people only."

A Southern white newspaperman measured, in an odd way, the importance of *The Souls of Black Folk* when he said, "This book is dangerous for the Negro to read, for it will only excite discontent and fill his imagination with things that do not exist or things that should not bear upon his mind." To young people, and especially to those individuals with undeveloped gifts in the creative arts, Du Bois' book struck a chord.

Boys and girls in the cotton fields of Alabama, in crowded slums of Chicago and New York, on the waterfront of New Orleans, began to pay attention to their dreams and to have pride in being Negroes. "By every civilized and peaceful method, we must strive for the rights which the world accords to men," wrote Du Bois. Words like these added inches to their height. It gave them a goal to use their special, individual gifts.

The words did something more. Dr. Du Bois ended one of his essays in this way: "And now behold a century new for the duty and the deed. The problem of the twentieth century is the problem of the color line."

J. Saunders Redding, a writer and leader in the movement for civil rights, points out that eighteen months after these words appeared in print, they were confirmed by the formation of the famous Niagara Movement—the forerunner of the National Association for the Advancement of Colored People. This organization was the first since the abolition movement to bring Negroes and white people together in equal striving for the American Dream.

The long years of silence in the face of terror and poverty and denial of true citizenship in their native land were at an end. With the opening of the twentieth century and the printing of a book, a new era of struggle had begun. A few young Negro Americans with the gift of words and art and music led the way.

I Have a Dream

1 / Lift Every Voice and Sing

Where is the Jim Crow section
On this merry-go-round,
Mister, cause I want to ride?
Down South where I come from
White and colored
Can't sit side by side.
Down South on the train
There's a Jim Crow car.
On the bus, we're put in the back—
But there ain't no back
To a merry-go-round!
Where's the horse
For a kid that's black?

LANGSTON HUGHES / *Merry-go-'round*

"Who am I?" If you were a girl or boy of African descent in the United States at the beginning of this century, your answer would probably have been "I am a Negro."

The words may have been spoken with a quiet, defiant pride, or the answer may have been given with downcast eyes. You would have been taught by circumstances out of your control that your dark skin was of more importance than your name, where you lived, your looks, or the role you hoped to play in the country of your birth. *I am a Negro*—and, in a world where the "somebodies" were white, that was almost like saying "I am a nobody."

Langston Hughes was a Negro American boy growing up at this time. He knew how it hurt to be set apart. When Hughes and the century were young, the word *Negro* summed up "all the bitter years of insult and struggle in America; the slave-beatings of yesterday; the lynchings, the Jim Crow cars, the only movie show in town with its sign: *For Whites Only*; the restaurants where you may not eat; the jobs you may not have; the unions you cannot join. . . ." Were hopes and dreams, then, all false? "Not so," Du Bois said, "the training in school is more needed than ever . . . above all the broader, deeper culture of gifted minds. . . . Will America be the poorer by fostering the talents of the Negro in conformity to the ideals of the American Republic?" This encouragement loosened tongues, and put pens in diffident hands.

In 1902, young James Weldon Johnson and his brother, in Jacksonville, Florida, had written down the notes and lyrics of a song which was published in New York It became a sort of national anthem expressing Negro hopes and needs. "Lift Every Voice and Sing" was only a beginning of fulfillment for the Johnson brothers. Eventually, they made their way north to New York to charm the theatre-going public with their lyric music. With them, the great migration of the gifted began.

Dr. Du Bois was soon to be on hand, editing the *Crisis*, a literary magazine published under the auspices of the newly-founded Association for the Advancement of Colored People. He opened its pages to the aspiring young Negro writers. A few years later, in 1923, the National Urban League, another interracial organization for bettering the lot of talented Negroes, founded the magazine *Opportunity*. Here, too, writers and artists were given an outlet for recognition. The poetry of Countee Cullen and Langston Hughes; the stories of Zora Neal Hurston; the blues set down by W. C. Handy; the drawings of Aaron Douglas—they made Harlem a magnet, pulling other aspiring and gifted young Negroes from the whole country.

Young Arna Bontemps came from California at this time. "In some places," he wrote much later, "the autumn of 1924 may have been an unremarkable season. In Harlem, it was like a foretaste of paradise. A blue haze descended at night and, with it, strings of fairy lights on the broad avenues. From the window of a small room in an apartment on Fifth Avenue and 129th Street, I looked over the roof tops of Negrodom and tried to believe my eyes. What a city! What a world!"

No longer was the answer to "Who Am I?" the inexorable, "I am a nobody because my skin is dark." Each was a person in his own right. Each had an identity, a name.

"In Harlem," Bontemps continued, "we were seen in a beautiful light. We were heralds of a dawning day. We were the first-born of the dark renaissance."

This new self-discovery of the talented Negro was centered in New York, but its influence did not stop at the shores of Manhattan Island.

When it all began, Roland Hayes was growing up in Chattanooga, Tennessee. Both of his parents had been slaves. His father, a carpenter on an Alabama plantation, had never had the opportunity to learn to read or write, but his mother had celebrated Emancipation in 1863 by learning to read. After her husband's death, she took in washing to earn enough to keep her sons in school.

When *The Souls of Black Folk* came out, Roland Hayes was an overgrown teenager working at odd jobs and using his beautiful tenor voice only in the church choir.

"Son," Fanny Hayes said, "you have a mission in life. You must use your singing for the uplift of our people."

Her words were but a translation of Du Bois' constant theme. Roland Hayes answered with years of struggle, first to get musical training and then to be accepted on the concert stage where no dark-skinned singer had stood before.

Henry Tanner, son of a Methodist bishop in Pennsylvania, came back from ten years studying in Paris, where his religious paintings already hung on famous museum walls, to begin the battle for recognition as an artist in his native country.

Paul Robeson, all-American athlete with a law degree from Harvard, found his true vocation on the stage and concert platform, but had a struggle to do so.

"By every civilized and peaceful method," they said, "we must strive for the rights which the world accords to men."

Up and down the land, the young people were stirred to think what they could do if they had the chance. Rich-

ard Wright, *lived* the wretchedness of *Black Boy* before
he escaped North to write history down. Arna Bontemps,
Jean Toomer, Claude McKay, Langston Hughes—one by
one the poets came. And the singers and dancers and musicians! Finding little money—barely enough to live on—
they found something better: acceptance of their own individual personalities in a world that no longer rejected
their gifts. *Who am I? I am myself, a Negro American
with something of value to give.*

Marian Anderson

"Your name, please?" The secretary of a conservatory of
music in Philadelphia jotted down a name and gave the
first student in line an application blank to fill out.

The line was quite long, even for the first registration
day of a new term.

"Next."

About the middle of the line stood a well-dressed young
girl, tall and dignified for her sixteen years. Like most of
the others, she wore a blue serge suit, high-buttoned patent
leather shoes, fresh white gloves, and a wide-brimmed
sailor hat. (Navy blue tailored suits, that spring of 1918,
were almost a uniform.) Noticing that the girl just ahead
had pulled off one glove, she did the same. When her turn
came, she held out her ungloved hand to receive the application blank. She gave her name, "Anderson, Marian
Anderson," in a low voice.

The young lady behind the desk looked right through
her and gestured impatiently to the next applicant to

come forward. When there was no one left in line, she glanced over coldly.

"What do *you* want?"

"An entry blank, please," the young applicant stammered.

"We don't take colored." There was neither contempt nor pity in the secretary's voice. She was simply stating a fact. The teachers at the conservatory did not accept Negro students.

"I don't think I said a word," Marian Anderson wrote in her autobiography many years later. "I just looked at this girl and was shocked that such words could come from one so young. . . . I could not conceive of a person surrounded with the joy that is music without having some sense of its beauty and understanding rub off on her. . . . It was as if a cold, horrifying hand had been laid on me."

Marian Anderson, wordless, turned slowly and walked out. *We don't take colored.* The words were mild, but the rejection cut very deep. "If it had happened in the South," she reasoned dolefully, "I could understand it."

She had made her first trip into Georgia from Philadelphia a few months earlier, to give a recital at one of the segregated private schools. She had been shocked and repelled by the dirty Jim Crow railroad cars they had traveled in and by the *White* and *Colored* signs, and had thanked heaven that she lived where no Jim Crow laws cut her off from all community life.

She was very upset by all she had seen in the South. And yet, there was one thing good she could say about it. It did have beautiful music.

Choirs of lovely voices from Southern schools had won fame in the North with their hymns and "sorrow songs" from slavery days. And on street corners, ragged boys with homemade instruments played complex melodies in a rhythm that made you want to dance. But not one of the girls in the school choirs with voices comparable to her own could ever dream of being trained in a conservatory, a privilege for which Marian Anderson had been saving every dollar she earned. You would expect to be turned away from a Southern conservatory, if you were crazy enough to go there. But this was her own Philadelphia!

Marian Anderson knew that Philadelphia was different from the South, and from most cities in the country. In the days before Emancipation, the "City of Brotherly Love" had been in the very center of struggle for freedom. But the fighting generation had grown old and passed away. Long before the turn of the century, the "old" families among the Philadelphia Negro population—like the Andersons—had developed normal roots in the community and had settled down to a comfortable existence.

Admittedly, they had the poorest jobs, the least money. In stores, they often had to stand around a long time waiting to be served. The street cars sometimes passed them by while they waited on the corner. But in the street cars, they could sit wherever they liked. All children attended the public schools in mixed neighborhoods without question. Negro Americans lived, as did most Philadelphians, except the very poor or the very wealthy, in narrow, red brick row houses within easy reach of schools, parks, and libraries. Children, at least, did not have to concern themselves with the outward signs of segregation.

Only a trickle of newcomers had moved in from the South. They were welcomed into the neighborhood life as Marian Anderson's mother had been when she came up from Virginia.

While Mr. Anderson had lived, he had supported the family by selling ice and coal and picking up odd jobs. On Sunday, he was an official in charge of ushers of the Union Baptist Church, where young Marian, from early childhood, had sung in the choir.

Mrs. Anderson had not worked. In Virginia, she had been a school teacher in a one-room country school for Negro children. When her husband died, she could not get a job in the Philadelphia schools. Though her three little girls could go to an integrated school, integration did not extend to the teaching staff. All the teachers were white. Only poorly paid domestic service was open to her. And, though later she found a job in a department store, it was still in a menial capacity. The little family had to move from their own home into the grandmother's already crowded three-story house.

Still, with all these problems and handicaps, Marian Anderson had a protected and happy childhood that centered around home and church—and music. Singing was the passion of her life.

Who am I? If Marian Anderson ever asked herself that question, the fact that she was a Negro, in a land where her people were second class citizens, would not have been her answer. From the age when she accompanied her songs on an imaginary piano, or learned the alto part of "Dear to the Heart of the Shepherd" for the Junior Sunday School Choir, she had but one answer for herself: "I am a singer."

She had had every reason to believe in her great gift,

every encouragement, until the rebuff at the music school. Even as a child, the members of her own church and of neighboring churches had arranged concerts for her. She was known as "The Ten-Year-Old Contralto." In high school, she sang solos in the glee club at school.

Roland Hayes, the most famous of Negro singers—the only one who was at this time known to the outside musical world as a concert artist—had praised her singing. The principal of the high school had said she had a voice worth training. At sixteen, she had to begin to think of ways of earning a living. If only she could do it by song! But suddenly, there was the training barrier: *We don't take colored.*

She did not try other music schools in the city. She did not intend to be hurt that way again. She told no one of the rejection except her mother, who counseled patience. The Andersons were not crusaders. "We don't go where we are not wanted," the older woman said, and the young girl agreed.

But an opportunity did come, just before Marian Anderson finished high school. One voice teacher in the neighborhood, Miss Mary Patterson, and then a Miss Agnes Reifsnyder, had given her private lessons. They taught her songs of Schubert and Brahms, and helped her arrange programs to include these as well as the spirituals she sang so well. But they were well aware that they could not give her the training her talent deserved.

Dr. Lucy Wilson, her high school principal, arranged through a friend, to have her sing for a well-known voice teacher, Guiseppi Boghetti. Mr. Boghetti had made it clear that he would hear her only as a favor, for he already had as many pupils as he could manage.

On the day of the audition, without much hope, Marian Anderson began the song she had chosen. It was "Deep River," a spiritual, a sorrow song of her people, one her father used to sing.

The stocky little Italian was visibly moved when she had finished. "I will make room for you right away," he said. "I will need only two years with you. After that, you will be able to sing anywhere and for anybody."

Two years with an expensive, first-rate teacher! Marian Anderson had saved up only enough money for a few lessons. Her Italian and Polish neighbors, and the devoted members of the Union Baptist Church, remedied that. They arranged a gala benefit concert for the girl they had watched growing up. Roland Hayes, who for twenty years had fought his way through the maze of prejudice and indifference to prove that a Negro musician could be a serious concert artist, was one of the soloists. The proceeds of that evening of love and faith—$600—were turned over to Mr. Boghetti for lessons. When that money was gone, he taught Marian Anderson for nothing.

She was soon singing at all the Negro colleges and private schools in the South, much as she dreaded Jim Crow traveling. She had won prizes and had sung with Roland Hayes in the Academy of Music in Philadelphia. She had even ventured a concert of her own at Town Hall in New York.

In spite of misgivings, she entered a contest to sing with the New York Philharmonic Orchestra at the Lewisohn Stadium, and won the coveted honor. This, her second appearance in New York, was a great success and brought her to the attention of one of the important concert managers, Arthur Judson. But the prejudice against serious

Negro singers was strong. Judson's management did not bring her many new engagements on the concert stage. Besides, the musical world was centered in Paris, in London, and in Milan, and a musical reputation required the acclaim of Europe first. Over there, musicianship was not judged by the color of an artist's skin. And, she was not satisfied that she was the finished musician her own standards required. A singer needed to know the languages in which the great songs of the Western Hemisphere were written. Mr. Boghetti could help her with Italian, but he could give her little help with the German language. And she loved the German songs of Schubert and Brahms and Schumann and Hugo Wolf. For training in German, she decided she would have to go abroad as Roland Hayes had done.

Marian Anderson spent first six months and then two years abroad. In 1935, her mother crossed the ocean to sit in the audience for her Paris triumph. Toscanini heard her sing in Salzburg, Austria, and told her, "Yours is a voice such as one hears once in a hundred years."

It was in Europe that Marian Anderson came to the attention of Sol Hurok, a major musical entrepeneur. With his backing, she came home to make a tour of the major cities of her own country. Step by step, under Hurok's management, the Philadelphia choir singer reached and surpassed the goals even she had set for herself. She divided her year between engagements in Europe, in England, Scandinavia, Finland, Russia, and her own country.

Great things were happening to the Negro people in America. Doors had opened in the arts, in government, in science—doors that once had seemed forever barred. In the middle thirties, Roland Hayes, Paul Robeson, and Marian Anderson ranked among the top ten serious concert artists in the United States. Miss Anderson rejoiced in the freer life, but she took no part in the struggle for that freedom. It was enough for her that she could sing.

Early in 1939, when she was a rose the continent in California, an echo of the words spoken in her girlhood came to trouble her serenity. This time, it was the ladies of the Daughters of the American Revolution in Washington, D. C., who said: *We don't take colored.* Sol Hurok had arranged a concert in the capital at Constitution Hall. But the D.A.R. owned the hall. And they canceled the concert.

Marian Anderson heard the rumor of the cancellation while she was in San Francisco. She was saddened, but assumed that Mr. Hurok would straighten things out. He was always careful to spare her any embarrassment. Then, on the way to her next concert, she saw a headline in the San Francisco paper: *Mrs. Roosevelt Takes Stand. Resigns from D.A.R.*

From city to city, as she made her way back across the continent, reporters tried to get Marian Anderson to comment. She would not. She kept hoping the excitement would die down. She shrank from being the center of a controversy. Surely there were other halls in Washington where the concert could be held. And if not Washington, some other city. . . .

But the excitement did not die down. The day had passed when prejudice against Negro artists could be ignored by black or by white Americans who shared the democratic dream.

Heifetz, the famous violinist, canceled his own concert

in Constitution Hall. "I could not play there," he said. "I am so ashamed." Other artists followed his lead.

A prominent woman in Birmingham, Alabama, who had never joined the D.A.R., now presented her credentials. She was admitted to the rolls of the "Daughters." But she had joined only for the porpose of resigning, which she did within the week.

Marian Anderson's name was on everybody's lips, but she did not welcome the publicity. She hated being looked on as a martyr, and felt sorrier for the people who had started the trouble than she did for herself.

"I would be fooling myself," she said, "to think that I was meant to be a fearless fighter. I was not, just as I was not meant to be a soprano instead of a contralto."

But fighter or not, the shy singer had become a symbol of freedom. Washington, in the era of Franklin Roosevelt, was full of people who refused to allow the insult to pass without protest. Many of them were Southerners. Mary McLeod Bethune, staunch fighter for equality for her people, was there from Florida. So was Charles Houston, the NAACP lawyer. Among the white Southerners was the Virginian, Oscar Chapman; Clark Foremen from Georgia, and Edwin Embree from Kentucky. His grandfather had been a bold Kentucky abolitionist. Senator Hugo Black, Aubrey Williams, and Virginia and Clifford Durr were from Alabama. It was people like these who hammered out a dramatic answer to the D.A.R.

First Oscar Chapman and Charles Houston consulted with Mrs. Roosevelt and Harold Ickes, Secretary of the Interior. Why not present Miss Anderson to the people of Washington at an outdoor concert on Easter Sunday? She could sing from the steps of the Lincoln Memorial. . . .

Marian Anderson was informed of the plan before the news was broadcast. Her consent did not come easily, but she realized that she had become a symbol of and for her people. She could not run from the situation, but she looked forward to Easter Sunday with misgivings. Might it not have been better if this had happened to somebody like Dr. DuBois, or Langston Hughes, Roland Hayes, or Paul Robeson? They gloried in the struggle. She only wanted to sing as well as a singer can.

But it had happened to *her* and, earnestly, she went ahead and planned a suitable program. She would begin with "My Country 'Tis of Thee." Then, an aria, perhaps "O Mio Fernando," followed by Schubert's "Ave Maria." And no concert of hers was complete without spirituals. From her large repertory, she chose "Gospel Train" and "Trampin' " and, for the ending, "My Soul is Anchored in the Lord."

With her mother, Miss Anderson made the trip from Philadelphia to Washington on Easter morning. No hotel in Washington would take them as guests, but they had known this ahead of time. They were met at the railroad station by ex-governor Gifford Pinchot of Pennsylvania and his wife, who drove them by the Lincoln Memorial where they checked the piano, the arrangements for Miss Anderson's accompanist, and the placing of the microphones on the platform. Then they drove to the Pinchot's home.

By noon, in the bright April sunshine, the crowds began to gather on the tree-dotted mall between the tall, inspiring shaft of the Washington Monument and the Memorial to Abraham Lincoln. Before the concert began, the audience extended from one hallowed spot to the other.

In the audience were a few old men and women who had been born in slavery, many more whose ancestors had inherited the scars and memories of that era. Great-grandchildren of slaves, in their Easter Sunday best, romped on the grass with the great-grandchildren of abolitionists and Union soldiers—and Confederate soldiers, too. The 75,000 who drew together in a semicircle between the Monument and the Memorial had come that day to help close the gap between the American Dream and the reality.

What were Marian Anderson's feelings then? She has told us a little of what she felt in her autobiography: "I had sensations unlike any I had experienced before. . . . My heart leaped wildly, and I could not talk. I even wondered whether I would be able to sing. . . . All I knew then, as I stepped forward, was the overwhelming impact of that vast multitude. I had a feeling that a great wave of good will poured out from these people, almost engulfing me. . . . I sang. I don't know how. . . . At the end, the tumult of the crowd's shouting would not die down."

For years afterward, strangers would come up after concerts in other cities to say with pride, "I was there. I heard you sing that Easter Sunday in Washington."

Eventually, Marian Anderson was to sing in the D.A.R.'s treasured Constitution Hall—at first, during World War II at a benefit performance. And then, at last, the policy was changed and she appeared in the hall as did any musical performer.

The Easter concert of 1939 did not serve to eliminate segregation. It did not even push every obstacle out of this great singer's path. But what it did do was to open a new page in the history of the struggle.

When Marian Anderson gave concerts in the South, not

all the care in the world could save her from the humiliations that came to all black Americans. In the auditoriums where she sang, Negroes who came to hear her were seated separately, in poorer seats. The separate cars on the railroads and the table in the dining car behind drawn curtains made her so uncomfortable, she rarely traveled except by automobile. Few Southern hotels welcomed her for overnight stops. She still stayed in private houses.

Though Marian Anderson's voice and training were equal to that of any operatic star—and she had already been invited to sing operatic roles in Scandinavia, in Italy, in Russia—the doors of the Metropolitan Opera in New York City were closed to her, and to other Negro artists, until near the end of her singing career.

"She has a glorious voice," opera fans said. "Too bad she's colored."

Then, in 1955, she was given a chance to become a member of the Metropolitan Opera Company. Her first role was as Ulrica in Verdi's opera, *The Masked Ball.*

She wrote of her opera experience: "The chance to be a member of the Metropolitan has been a highlight of my life. It has meant much to me and to my people. If I have been privileged to serve as a symbol, to be the first Negro to sing as a regular member of the Metropolitan company, I take greater pride from knowing that the doors everywhere may open increasingly to those who have prepared themselves well. . . ."

Quite late in life, Marian Anderson had married King Fisher, a successful architect. Together, they had created a beautiful and secluded home on a Connecticut hillside. Here, in 1965, Marian Anderson planned her retirement.

She thought back over the years of her life, recalling the many talented people besides herself who had won the opportunity to be themselves, to use their gifts, and wondered why progress had taken so long. "There are many persons ready to do what is right because in their hearts they know it is right. But they hesitate, waiting for the other fellow to make the first move—and he, in turn, waits for you. . . . Not everyone can be turned aside from meanness and hatred, but the great majority of Americans is heading in that direction. I have a great belief in the future of my people and my country."

Marian Anderson understood herself very well when she said that she was not a crusader. But history took a hand and, it can truly be said that, on the day of the memorable March on Washington, August 1963, when she sang again from the steps of the Lincoln Memorial, that she sang for her people's freedom.

2 / For Life, Liberty, and the Pursuit of Jobs

O, yes,
I say it plain,
America never was America to me,
And yet I swear this oath—
America will be!
An ever-living seed,
Its dream
Lies deep in the heart of me.

LANGSTON HUGHES / Let America Be America Again

As the century progressed, it was clear that for every Negro singer, artist, essayist, and novelist who, by their talents, achieved some dignity as human beings, tens of thousands of their fellow Negroes were still being shunted off the highroad of American life. The fame of singers, poets, and novelists had dispelled, to a certain degree, the cruel myth that the Negro was an inferior human being. An essayist and historian such as W. E. B. Du Bois could open chapters of forgotten history. These new spokesmen of the Negro people were widely read and listened to—at least in the Northern cities.

Members of the white world were moved to pity and indignation when they read Claude McKay's bitter cry against the brutalities of race riots and lynchings, or Richard Wright's account of his own Mississippi childhood in *Black Boy*. They applauded the Negro songs born of sorrow and suffering heard in concert halls where Negroes were not admitted. But songs were not enough, words and poetry were not enough to change the condition of millions of Americans with dark skins and the heritage of slavery. Even when they escaped to search for freedom in Northern cities, the poison of prejudice followed them.

Even if they managed to get the education and training for responsible, well-paying jobs or professions, there was always the stop sign: *For whites only*. Sympathetic white teachers in the public schools discouraged their pupils from taking a college entrance course. It seemed cruel, they explained, when college degree or not, young Negroes would end up earning a living as janitors, elevator operators, or household servants.

Most discouraging of all was the attitude of skilled white working men and women. Through banding together in unions, many workers had won the right to bargain for better wages and working conditions; but the unions almost never admitted a Negro to membership. In the heavy industries such as steel mills and automobile factories, where many Negroes found jobs, unions had not yet been recognized as bargaining agents for the workers. The hundreds of thousands of Negro workers lived without protection of unions, and on the edge of poverty.

In 1929, the era of post-war prosperity faded abruptly. The great economic depression set in. The plight of Negro Americans became distressingly clear. In the industrial centers and in the rural South alike, they suffered first and longest.

Four years passed. Franklin Delano Roosevelt became President. With him, a well-meaning national government came to power, but proved helpless to provide equal opportunities for work in the North and equal economic assistance in the South. The Negro leaders now heard apologies for injustice; regrets that, because of laws and the custom of segregation, the Negroes had to go to poorer schools; that grown men and women were denied the right to vote, and denied the right to use their skills in the workaday world. Telling the story of the Negro in poetry and drama and song had not proved enough to break down the prejudice and indifference of the past.

"Who would be free, themselves must strike the blow," Frederick Douglass, escaped slave and abolitionist, had said during the Civil War. Not only the few with special talents in the arts but the millions of plain working people must act on their own behalf before "America could be America." The Negro artists and writers, the leaders of what Arna Bontemps had called the "dark renaissance," now realized this to their sorrow. Among the first and most important to call for mass action to secure the equal opportunity to work was a Southerner who, like others, had been drawn to New York "as to a paradise!" His name was Asa Philip Randolph.

Asa Philip Randolph

"Do you have any work I can do, Mister?" Philip Randolph had been asking that question since he was ten years old. Jobs! He had been looking for jobs as long as he could remember.

In Crescent City, the small town in northeast Florida where he was born; in Jacksonville, where he went alone at the age of fifteen to get a high school education at Cookman Institute; he had looked for any work that would earn money. There were, in 1904, no public high schools for Negroes in all of Florida. The few young boys who aspired to an education above the sixth grade went to Cookman, the girls to Mrs. Mary McLeod Bethune's school farther down the coast.

Randolph's parents had been born in Virginia in the time of slavery and, after Emancipation, had received the beginnings of an education in the tent schools. In later years, when Philip's father had become a Methodist minister, they moved to Florida into the parsonage of the small and struggling A.M.E. Zion church in Crescent City. Here, in perpetual poverty, they had brought up two sons. Mrs. Randolph ran a small dry cleaning and mending business in the backyard of the parsonage.

Even though young Randolph managed to earn his own way at Cookman Institute, it was a sacrifice for the family to spare his meager earnings when he left home. But education was a symbol of the freedom promised by the United States Constitution, by the Emancipation Proclamation, and by the Bible. Both parents were agreed that the boy must have the best available. Mrs. Randolph assured her son that they'd manage without the dimes and quarters he had brought home from selling newspapers and running errands at the village grocery. Maybe there'd be better jobs, as well as learning, in the city of Jacksonville.

The jobs in Jacksonville had been different—and a lot harder. All through his years at Cookman, young Randolph had dug ditches and laid cross-ties for the new railroad that was being built to attract white tourists to the seacoast.

When his schooling was over, and the railroad built, the tall, lanky student headed for New York City. New York wasn't entirely strange to him. He had been there for a short while two summers earlier and had earned good money as a hall boy, tending door and running the elevator in a big apartment house on West Seventieth Street. The hours were long, but he had time on the job to read books from the Public Library. (To a young Negro from the South, being able to borrow books from a library was, itself, a miracle.) In New York, there'd be hours to spare from earning a living. There would be good colleges to go to. In New York, he would have a chance to become a writer, or maybe an orator—to speak for "The Race" on street corners or in meeting halls. From babyhood, he had listened to his father practicing sermons. And young Phil Randolph had had some success in debating at Cookman and he had heard John Hope of Atlanta and Mrs. Bethune using words as weapons in the battle for a better life for Negro Americans. Eloquence and a good voice could move people—if you had something to say—and Philip Randolph felt within himself a deep confidence in his abilities.

His parents had fostered this confidence in ways they knew best. On the day he left home for the Cookman Institute, his father had put *The Souls of Black Folk* into his hands along with a Bible. Dog-eared and almost worn out now, The Du Bois book was in the pocket of Randolph's jacket when he got on the train to go north. It had given him words to express his own thoughts, had given form to his vague desire to speak or write, and was drawing him, like a magnet, to the city where writers saw their work in print.

Philip Randolph dreamed his future all the way north in the Jim Crow railroad car. But when he found himself on the crowded streets of the big city, the nineteen-year-old stowed his dreams in the back of his mind. First, a man had to find a way to live. He made his way to the West Seventieth Street neighborhood again. A job as elevator man would do to begin. He turned at random into the covered entrance of a building and pressed the superintendent's bell.

"Do you have any work I can do, Mister?"

Ten minutes later, Philip Randolph, a young man with a brilliant mind and better-than-usual high school education, had a broom in his hand. He was to sweep the sidewalk. To the white superintendent who had hired him, this was an appropriate job for the "likely colored boy." It didn't matter to Randolph. He was in New York and he was on his way!

In the years between 1908 and 1915, Randolph made his

living as elevator operator and hall boy, as a porter in the big Consolidated Edison Building, as waiter and cook on the Fall River Line of excursion boats. Doing work of this kind, he met other aspiring writers, artists, thinkers with dark skins. Some of them had had work published, many had advanced college degrees. But when it came working for wages, service jobs were all that they could find.

One year after Philip Randolph came north, the National Association for the Advancement of Colored People was formed. Two years later, the National Urban League, another interracial organization, whose purpose was to improve the job situation for capable young Negroes, came into being. Dr. Du Bois had already started publishing the NAACP magazine, the *Crisis*. Charles Johnson, of the Urban League also encouraged Negro writers by publishing their work in the monthly journal, *Opportunity*. Around the *Crisis* especially, talented young Negroes clustered, finding the answer to "Who Am I," voicing in print the aspirations of an oppressed people.

Philip Randolph was one of this group, though he had done no writing. He went to night classes at City College for several years, taking courses in economics, political science, philosophy, and English. Words were still his fascination—words, spoken or written. But he had to make up his mind about a lot of things and he took his time.

A teacher at the college, Dr. Morris Cohen, took a special interest in Philip Randolph, as he did with many of his unusual students. Dr. Cohen was one of those rare teachers whose influence on their students extends far beyond the classroom. As Du Bois had set Philip Randolph's goals with a book, so Morris Cohen guided the young man's interest toward deep consideration of long-term, many-sided solutions for the problems of the Negro American.

Randolph had come vaguely in search of freedom to develop his own personality, in order to know the world and himself. His father had tried to give his son a pride in being Negro. His mother had impressed upon him the freedom every human being must have to use his own talents. Now, after five years, Randolph asked himself: "Just what is meant by Freedom?" Surely not just the chances given to what Du Bois called the "Talented Tenth" to prove to themselves and the world that not *every* Negro was inferior to every white man! The artists and musicians, the medical men and ministers and engineers were important; they had every right to develop their individual gifts. But the concept *freedom* was not meant just for a few leaders. It meant the right of plain ordinary men and women to work at plain ordinary jobs of their own choosing. Those who wanted to become craftsmen—bricklayers, plasterers, plumbers—had a right to learn these skills and work at them at the same wages paid to others. They had a right to join unions and to work for better wages and decent working conditions.

Randolph went further in his thinking. He had come to believe that those who did the work in this world really created the wealth and, therefore, ought to control the land and natural resources, the mines, the water power and electrical plants, the railroads and huge factories. This is to say that, politically, Philip Randolph became a socialist.

"We have to be free in order to be equal," he announced to a friend one evening over a cup of coffee in a Harlem cafeteria, "and we have to be equal in order to be free." He spoke with a sense of wonder, as if he had made an astounding discovery.

Owen Chandler, the young law student across the table, laughed. "That's what I've been telling you. What are you going to do about it?"

The question brought Philip Randolph up short. Five years had gone by since he stepped off the northbound train, a penniless country boy from Florida. He was penniless still, and wanting to get ahead so that he could marry the girl he was in love with, wanting, even more, to do something for his people. For all his studying, he had no college degrees, no profession. He had written nothing, had done no public speaking except to give readings of other people's poetry in Negro churches. (At Professor Cohen's suggestion, he had taken lessons in public speaking. His instructor happened to be an Englishman from Oxford University and, under this training, his own soft, slurring Southern speech had given way to the clipped, precise accent of his teacher—the accent that was to stay with him for the rest of his life.)

"Do about it? I haven't even got a job."

"Fired? Again?"

Randolph saw the consternation in Owen Chandler's face and shrugged. He had trouble keeping jobs because, wherever he was, he talked union to the workers. He had been trying for a year to get elevator operators to form a union. He had a few signed up, but they had no charter, no recognition, had made no demands. Yet, when the bosses heard the word "union," they were outraged.

"The boss thought I was 'too smart to fall for that radical union stuff.' He talked to me like a father. Then he fired me on the spot." Randolph stirred his coffee thoughtfully. "Maybe it's a good time to stop fooling around with jobs like that. What I'd like to do is to start a paper, begin talking aloud to the plain ordinary people with plain ordinary jobs. Mass organization—mass action—I'd explain it in language people would understand."

"Why don't you? Phil, you've got something."

"Got something? I haven't even got money enough to buy the paper to print Volume I, Number I."

Owen Chandler leaned forward, his eyes aglow. "I've got a little money saved. We can borrow more."

"You're in law school. You're going to be a lawyer." Randolph objected.

"I *was* studying law," Chandler said. "The message you want to get across is more important. I can manage the business end and you can do the writing and editing."

So, over a table in a shabby little cafeteria in Harlem, *The Messenger* was born. The year was 1915. A year when there were still more horse-drawn vehicles on the streets than motor cars; when moving pictures were a tremendous sensation to be seen at nickelodeons, if you had the five cents entrance fee; when women in daring ankle-length skirts paraded city streets demanding the vote. A year when school boys wore knickers and long black stockings; and girls, listening to phonograph records playing "Alexander's Ragtime Band" read *Pollyana*. The year that Booker T. Washington died in Alabama.

The European nations had been at war with one another for months. Like Dr. Du Bois, Randolph and his friends saw the struggle as rivalry for the opportunity to rule over the dark people in Asian and African colonies—rivalry turning to violence. Negro Americans saw justice neither in the German claims to rule the world nor in the claims of the British and their allies to hold on to colonies.

More important to the Negro American was the vast migration from the plantations of the South when the cotton crop was ruined for two years in succession by a little bug called the boll weevil. Thousands of tenant farmers and sharecroppers from Georgia and Alabama, from South Carolina and Mississippi, were jobless, without food to eat or even a leaky roof over their heads. The Northern cities became the Promised Land to which they turned longing eyes. More Negroes had left the South in 1915 to look for work and for the breath of freedom than in the days of slavery and the Underground Railroad.

In comparison to the poverty and injustices they suffered at home, the crowded slums offered a kind of freedom. But in Philip Randolph's opinion, it was no more than freedom from terror and starvation. The newcomers brought with them a crushing belief, implanted by the contempt of white Southerners, that they were, indeed, inferior. Because they had never been permitted to have a share in the government, most did not register or vote even in New York where the vote was open to them. Because they had been denied education, most were poorly prepared to claim any place in the world of science and arts opening around them.

These were the "masses" Philip Randolph and Owen Chandler dreamed of reaching with *The Messenger*— these ragged newcomers at the very bottom of the ladder.

Like a farmer sowing seed in freshly plowed land, month after month, Randolph planted his ideas, his determination, his hope.

"Negroes," he wrote over and over again, "must be free

in order to be equal, and they must be equal in order to be free."

"*The colored people of America want the cause of democracy to march forward. They want the Brotherhood of Man to triumph. They want security and plenty with freedom. They want political, economic and social equality.*

"*Will this come? It will only come if the downtrodden people fight for it.*"

How could they fight? With what weapons? Randolph reminded his readers that Frederick Douglass had said fifty years ago: *Who would be free, themselves must strike the blow.* The first blow, in his America of 1925, was to be economic opportunity.

He wrote that ninety-nine per cent of the Negro people were workers who sold their labor for wages, and that what the Negro had most of was his ability to work. But the Negro, Randolph said, was met everywhere by the barrier of color. The answer, according to Randolph, was that Negro workers had to find an equal place with whites in organized labor unions. Together, white and colored, could win decent wages to buy the goods their work had created. Strong unions, in his opinion, were the weapon that would win a better world.

But jobs, he pointed out, were only one weapon which the Negro people could use in their fight for liberation. Political action was needed to *unmake* the situation created by three hundred years of slavery and second class citizenship.

For years, *The Messenger,* edited and, for the most part, written by Randolph, came out month by month. The writing was forceful, the ideas solid. The paper helped to build self-respect in the masses of Negro American workers. Randolph's constant plea for mass organization in labor unions began to bear fruit.

Two years after he started *The Messenger*, Randolph finally succeeded in organizing a union among elevator operators, though it never was strong as a bargaining agent.

In 1925, the men and women who worked as Pullman porters and maids asked Randolph to help them organize a union. He had convinced them, with his writing, that unions were important. Every other branch of workers on the railroads were organized—engineers, brakemen, firemen, conductors. Only the Pullman porters and maids had no one to speak for them.

To Philip Randolph, this did not seem to be an assignment very different from many he had worked on. He was already considered a labor leader. He accepted; transformed *The Messenger* into the organ representing the "Brotherhood of Sleeping Car Porters and Maids," and set out confidently to organize. He soon discovered that he had a tiger by the tail! The officials of the Pullman Company, which built luxurious sleeping cars and leased them to the railroads, liked things as they were. For years, they fought furiously against change. The Pullman porters had very little money; the company was enormously wealthy. The hard times that had set in so soon after Randolph began his new job only made things worse. In the depression, few people traveled, fewer still rode in Pullman cars. Over half of the Pullman porters were without jobs. There was no such thing as social security or unemployment insurance. Those who were still employed, worked irregularly, sometimes only a few days a month. But Randolph kept going and, when Franklin Delano

Roosevelt was elected President in 1932, things began to change.

New laws were passed, favorable to the unionization of laboring people; a new feeling about the rights of working people, black and white, began to emerge in the federal government. Negroes began to vote in greater numbers and to have more say in the government. This had an effect on the officials of the Pullman Company, especially after the union was brought under the Railway Labor Act. And so, the officials tried to bribe Philip Randolph to abandon the fight.

One day, he received a check in the mail for five thousand dollars, with a friendly note suggesting that, since he worked so hard and so long, he needed a vacation. Perhaps, the letter suggested, he and his wife would enjoy a trip abroad.

Wouldn't he! Philip Randolph stared at the check. He needed money badly, and that month didn't even know how his rent would be paid; but the check went back to the Pullman Company in the next mail. Abandoning a struggle he had undertaken was the last thing Randolph would consider. The Company resisted a few months longer, but early in 1937, twelve years after he had begun the fight, Philip Randolph, for the Brotherhood of Sleeping Car Porters and Maids, signed a contract with the Pullman Company. A living wage. Fair hiring practices. The dignity of the individual worker. "The boss won't listen when one man squawks, but he has to listen when the union talks," says a union song.

As spokesman for an important union affiliated with the American Federation of Labor (A.F. of L.), Randolph was listened to with respect in the nation's capital and in his own city. The mayor of New York City, in these years before World War II, was Fiorello La Guardia. La Guardia, a warm supporter of the equality of all citizens, offered Randolph a position in the city government. The offer was tempting, but other Negroes were in the government and would continue to fight for Negroes to be represented, for their direct participation in government. Randolph was one of the few Negro leaders in the labor unions, and he believed what the Negro Americans needed most was jobs.

New industrial unions had come into existence after a bloody struggle. Banded together in the Congress of Industrial Organization, the C.I.O. admitted Negro Americans to equal membership. The older craft unions, with which the Brotherhood of Sleeping Car Porters and Maids was affiliated, still practiced discrimination. Because workers must eat, the fight for jobs had first priority in Randolph's mind. He saw that, in spite of the policy of the C.I.O. against discrimination, Negro men and women were still being hired for the lowest paid and least desirable jobs. And in the A.F. of L. craft unions, there were no openings at all. In spite of all the welfare measures of the New Deal government, thousands upon thousands of black Americans were unemployed.

To be free we must be equal and to be equal we must be free. This was still his constant refrain.

Again, in 1939, war had broken out in Europe. Hitler in Germany and Mussolini in Italy had crushed labor unions, murdered thousands of their own freedom-loving people, and now were joined together with the avowed purpose of conquering their neighbors. Second class citizenship and discrimination in its most violent form was spreading over the world. The United States was turned into what Roosevelt called "an arsenal of democracy," sending planes and ships and guns overseas to stave off a victory of the fascist forces.

Philip Randolph, all his life a pacifist, believed in nonviolent action to settle differences between nations as well as between individuals. Nevertheless, he saw that this war was not like other wars. He pointed out that Hitler talked of "master races," of the insignificance of the individual, of slavery. These were things thirteen million Negro Americans understood all too well. Fascism, he saw, must be defeated. But, while standing against racial bigotry across the ocean, American Negroes could, in Randolph's opinion, do no greater service to their own country than to keep up the struggle for equality at home.

He saw a million young Negro men drafted into the Army and Navy. In 1940 and 1941, thousands were pouring out of the South to get jobs in the defense plants and shipyards in the North and West. And he saw them being put into *segregated* training camps in the Army, in the galleys as messmen on ships of the Navy and Merchant Marine. He saw them turned away at the factory doors, or if admitted, put to work at "Negro jobs"—sweeping floors or cleaning restrooms.

Was this the way to fulfill the promise of the Declaration of Independence and the Constitution? Could America become "an arsenal of democracy" when willing workers were denied the right of other Americans? This was no time, in Philip Randolph's opinion, to carry on the struggle in the old, slow ways of education, persuasion, and legal action. For the leaders of the old organizations

merely to speak out was not enough. For the federal government to counsel patience was not enough. No words
were enough—unless they were the words of the man in
the White House. An order from President Roosevelt, as
commander-in-chief, could give equal treatment, equal
opportunity in the armed forces. An order from President
Roosevelt, as chief executive, could open the doors of the
defense plants and the hiring halls in the shipyards.

But the Negroes themselves must make the demands.

It was a daring plan. Almost singlehandedly, Philip
Randolph launched the March on Washington Movement. Negro Americans responded to the call for mass
action. The NAACP, The National Urban League, the
Negro churches, the Voters' Leagues—became part of the
movement. But Randolph put his dependence on the great
mass of workers in and out of the unions. He had sensed
what they wanted and needed: bread and a chance to use
the abilities so long denied them by white America. Huge
rallies were held. A date was set for the March.

Randolph, at first, had set the goal at ten thousand men
and women converging on Washington from the North,
the South, the East, and West. He raised the number to
a hundred thousand. There seemed no limit to the number who would come. Only Negroes were to be in this
march, not because Randolph was anti-white, but because
he felt this was, peculiarly, the Negro's own job. *Who
would be free, themselves must strike the blow.*

As the day approached, news articles and editorials in
the newspapers, radio commentators, and white ministers
all began talking of the dangers of so large a gathering.
They called it revolution, anarchism, a threat to the war
effort. Before this, only the Negro-owned newspapers had

mentioned the March on Washington. For them, from the beginning, Randolph's March had been front page news. White allies—even such staunch friends as Fiorella La Guardia and Mrs. Roosevelt—begged Randolph to give up the idea. But organized mass action was not a sudden whim. It had been in his mind for twenty years. Nothing else would have an equal effect.

As over the years, his answer was the same. Mass action placed human beings in physical motion that can be seen and heard and felt. Nothing less could change public sentiment. Negotiations had failed. Persuasion had failed. This demonstration against Jim Crow would get the attention the problem deserved. He refused to call off the March. To Mrs. Roosevelt, he said, "I'm certain it will do some good. In fact it has already done some good; for if you were not concerned about it, you wouldn't be here now."

Yet, the March did not take place. A week before the date set, Philip Randolph, with Walter White of the NAACP and T. S. Hill, head of the National Urban League, were invited to the White House to confer with President Roosevelt.

The President was not his usual jovial self. He looked worried. "We cannot have a March on Washington," he said. "We must approach the problem in another way."

"Then something will have to be done at once, Mr. President." Philip Randolph spoke without heat, but without hesitation. It would be too bad if the March disrupted and delayed the vast effort to prepare for war. But, the lives of African-Americans had been disrupted for generations, and justice to them had been too long delayed.

"Call off the March. Something will be done."

The promise of action by the President was welcome. But Philip did not give an inch. "Something must be done *now*."

Turning to Walter White, whom he knew better than Randolph, Roosevelt asked slowly, "How many will *really* march, Walter?"

The answer came after a quick glance at Randolph's stern face. "At least one hundred thousand, Mr. President."

Roosevelt leaned forward slightly in his chair and stared for a moment into the somber eyes of the union leader.

"What do you want me to do?"

Philip Randolph replied slowly. This was the big moment of his life. "Issue an executive order, Mr. President, banning discrimination in war industries."

Almost everything in 1941 was a war industry, from the garment workers making uniforms for soldiers instead of ladies' dresses, to the huge automobile factories with tanks and army trucks on the assembly line, and airplane plants and shipyards turning out fighter planes and battleships.

"An executive order from you, sir, and a committee with Negro members on it for enforcement."

"I'll do it." The famous, warm smile suddenly broke through Franklin Roosevelt's worried look. He held his hand out across the desk and clasped Randolph's in his. He had met a man with courage and determination to match his own.

Five days later, on June 25, 1941, the famous Executive Order 8802 was issued and, on the same day, Philip Randolph called off the March.

The executive order to end discrimination in hiring workers in defense industries, and the Fair Employment

Practices Committee appointed to oversee its enforcement, was a war measure, though its rulings did not extend to the armed services. Its importance to Negro workers after December 7, 1941, when the United States declared war on Germany, Italy, and Japan, can scarcely be overestimated. For this was the first time, since the Reconstruction era, that the federal government had intervened in behalf of the Negroes—but not the last. It is true that enforcement, especially in the South, was anything but perfect; nevertheless, resistance to the order fell before the great need for war workers, even in the deep South, and men and women who never before had had an opportunity to prove their skill won positions of responsibility. And the Negro American himself learned an important lesson— non-violent militant action pays off!

The National March on Washington Movement did not disband with this first great victory. Philip Randolph knew that "freedom is a hard-bought thing." In mass meetings all over the country, Negroes showed by their presence that they were ready to take up mass action whenever it seemed necessary. The March was postponed, not abandoned. More than twenty years later, it took place. Not for Negro Americans alone in 1963, and not with a mere hundred thousand marchers. Two hundred and fifty thousand Americans—black and white together—came to Washington, at last, in the greatest assembly for redress of wrongs that the people of the United States had ever witnessed.

"The advance guard of a revolution." This is what Randolph called it. With another long-time believer in non-violent mass action, Bayard Rustin, Philip Randolph was

the moving spirit and director of the 1963 March. Seventy-five years old, but tall, straight, and handsome as ever, he walked at the head of the mammoth line. As he stood on the platform, with the statue of Abraham Lincoln visible within the Memorial behind him, there was a likeness in the look of the eyes of the statue and the man. They were the eyes of a man who, from his youth, had tried to carry forward the promise of freedom and equality. They were tired eyes, wondering eyes, that looked into the blurred mass of faces upturned and saw the visible proof of an old dream come true.

Mass, non-violent action for freedom. W. E. B. Du Bois had had the dream before Randolph. On the platform beside him was a young minister from Georgia who had dreamed the dream anew—Martin Luther King, Jr.

Philip Randolph was seventy-five and tired. But his message to that listening throng displayed no sign of that weariness. It was, "There must be no relaxation if we hope to be a free people."

Randolph himself did not for a moment relax in his struggle for equal rights for all Americans, even after the triumphant March was over. He recognized the event as a milestone, not the end of the road. Through the summer and fall of 1963, the lawlessness against the civil rights protest continued unabated. In the Congress, the Civil Rights Bill demanded by the Marchers hung in the limbo of the rules committee. Demonstrators North and South picketed and sang Freedom Songs from the cells of Southern—and Northern—jails. They won growing numbers of white allies to the cause but not enough, and a few "summer patriots" fell away. At a moment of discouragement in the nation, President John F. Kennedy made a gracious and meaningful gesture for human rights by establishing a Freedom Medal as the highest honor that could be bestowed on civilians. In October, 1963, the distinguished recipients were invited to the White House. Among their number was Asa Philip Randolph who, for forty years, had been saying to American Negroes—"We have to be free in order to be equal and we have to be equal in order to be free."

3 / *Freedom on the Seas*

"How Democracy, with desperate vengeful port, strides on, shown through the dark by those flashes of lightning!"

WALT WHITMAN / *"Rise, oh days, from your fathomless depths"*

The first American to be killed in the Boston Massacre in 1770, the opening struggle of the Revolution, was a fugitive slave, a seaman on the waterfront, Crispus Attucks. Negroes and whites, side by side, defended the bridge at Concord and the village green at Lexington, Massachusetts. Black soldiers and white went through the starvation winter at Valley Forge. Only in South Carolina and Georgia, where the awful myth of white supremacy, the belief that *any* white European-American was better than *any* black African-American, had taken too firm a hold —only in those colonies was the Negro American denied the right to fight for his country's freedom in the Revolutionary War.

The small war against England in 1812 was fought mostly at sea. Negro sailors this time were welcomed in defense of the rights of their newly formed nation.

It was not until the Civil War was two years old, and only at the insistent demand of Fredrick Douglass and his fellow abolitionists, that the free Negroes of the North and the enslaved in the South were enlisted to fight for an end to slavery. Even then, the 200,000 Negro soldiers in the uniform of the United States were segregated in separate regiments, led by white officers.

Prejudice because of color and ancestry had not yet extended to the ships at sea. When a South Carolina slave, Robert Smalls, left on night-watch duty by his captain-master, sailed the Confederate ship out to join the United States fleet blockading Southern waters, he was made a Captain in the Union Navy. There was no rule against enlistment of Negro patriots for service in the Navy. That came later, and was (except for messmen and stokers) in full force at the time of World War II.

On the home front, after President Roosevelt's Executive Order 8802, Negro Americans from the South poured into Northern and Western cities to work at building tanks and trucks and ships and fighting planes in defense against the enemy. Even in the factories and mines and shipyards of the South, the President's Order enabled working people to take a rightful place "without regard to color or race."

Still, the Navy and the Merchant Marine, whose ships carried supplies and troops through the dangerous waters, remained segregated. Soldiers, drafted to fight and perhaps die for their country, were pushed (as they had been in World War I) into all-Negro battalions. The training camps were mostly in the South and were Jim Crow, down to the buses that took the draftees to town when they had a pass. The life-saving blood plasma from Red Cross blood banks was segregated even though Dr. Charles Richard Drew, a Negro scientist, had made its use possible.

The irony was not lost on the Negro soldiers. Whereas in Revolutionary times, black and white men fought side by side, during World War II, segregation was the rule rather than the exception. Finally, however, largely due to the demands raised by Philip Randolph's March on Washington Movement, qualified Negro Americans were enrolled in unsegregated training camps for Army officers. More than six thousand Negro officers were commissioned, and one—Benjamin O. Davis—was made a general; but still no officers of African or Asian descent were in positions of command on naval vessels.

Late in 1942, Negro Americans were permitted to enlist as sailors on warships, although none received commissions.

In the Merchant Marine, however, the barrier of color was broken down through the united efforts of labor unions, concerned individuals, and one persistent seaman —Hugh Mulzac.

Hugh Mulzac

The streets of the seacoast town of Wilmington, North Carolina, were Sunday quiet. At the end of a main street, a church raised its single, glistening white spire. The wooden building, freshly painted, was not handsome but to the young man striding beside Captain Granderson, the church, the town, the unimportant street, and the flower-fragrant air of a mild April morning itself were touched with storybook glamour. It was Hugh Mulzac's first sight of the North American mainland, a wonder world of wealth and opportunity. The year was 1907, and young Hugh had just turned twenty-one.

The barque *Aeolus*, on which he had sailed as an ordinary seaman, had come to port after a three week's voyage from the Caribbean Island of Barbados. She had lowered sails and docked at twilight. All hands had stayed aboard through the night, but the captain had gone into town. A pious man, he had promised to locate a good Protestant church so that his men—"Any who wished to," he added rather wistfully, since he knew that not many aboard were religious—could enjoy a real Sunday service in his company.

He reported back. "It's not like Oslo, to be sure. But North Carolina is good Christian country." To Hugh Mulzac, who had been so faithful at the numerous prayer meetings during the voyage, he added, "You will hear Scripture read and a sermon that will please the heart. See that you get your best clothes ready." Young Hugh had brought no Sunday suit along, but he was as neatly dressed as any of the others.

The church bell was tolling as the six seaman—the mate, sailmaker, the bos'un, the deck boy, Captain Granderson, and Hugh Mulzac—walked up to the open door. As was fitting, Mulzac fell back to let the chief mate and the bos'un follow Captain Granderson into the cool darkness. He was, after all, the youngest and least experienced of the crew.

One by one the others filed in. As Mulzac waited his turn, the first notes of *Rock of Ages* came to his ears. The service was under way. Savoring the moment, storing the memory as he had so many others on this, his first voyage beyond the islands, he started to follow the deck boy across the threshold. A heavy arm barred his way, and a drawling voice asked where he thought he was going.

"Why, to church, sir," he answered, in his precise English accent.

"Not in this church, you're not. Don't you know the law?"

By this time, Captain Granderson had come out to see the cause of the delay.

"This young man is with me," Granderson explained. "I've brought him from Barbados in the West Indies. I'm Captain Granderson of the barque *Aeolus* out in the harbor. The lad's very religious. His grandfather was a minister of the Gospel."

There was anger in the answering voice, and a contempt such as Mulzac had not met with before. "This is North Carolina. We're a state that believes in law and order."

"Is there a reason one of my crew can't join me at worship?"

"Segregation, that's why. White and black don't mix here."

A small crowd of passers-by had gathered and the curate came out of the church. Sick with humiliation, the young West Indian sailor listened while the curate explained to Granderson that a segregation law forbade Negroes and whites to worship together in the state of North Carolina.

"I'll tell you what we'll do. You can all go in and sit down. The colored boy can go up in the balcony—the old slave gallery. We haven't used it for years, of course. Our Negroes have their own churches in colored town. Yes, the balcony will do nicely."

"Oh, no it won't," Captain Granderson stormed. "If Hugh goes up there, we all go. The law is it? And what about Christianity?"

Hugh Mulzac would have given anything to turn and leave the church, leave the shores of the mainland forever. But Captain Granderson had already called out the other sailors and was climbing the rickety balcony stairs.

Hugh Mulzac sat through the service in the old slave gallery of the Wilmington church in complete wretchedness. Of course, his skin was dark, his eyes brown, and his hair stiffly curly, but he had never before in his twenty-one years thought of himself as different—no more so than Johnny, the Swedish deck boy, was different from Blackie, the Irish sailmaker. *Segregation*, that man had called it. With all his being, Hugh Mulzac hated the word.

His mother's father, as Captain Granderson had said, had been a minister. His paternal grandfather had come to the Islands from Scotland in the 1870's, had married a prim native girl who looked like a black Queen Victoria. Mulzac had bought a small island and started raising cotton and cattle—and a family. His mother's family, proud of her African ancestry, was from a nearby island. By the time young Hugh was old enough to remember anything, it seemed to him that half the people on Union Island were Mulzacs. And the other half, white and Negro, worked for the family. The church was his grandfather's church as long as he lived. His Scottish grandfather taught the school. They lived in an eight-room house made of wood. The workers, who were not in the family, lived in mud huts. There was, otherwise, no difference between them.

Even when he was sent to St. Vincent's Island to finish his education, Hugh Mulzac had not been made to feel any different because of his color. The differences were between the rich and the poor. But, because his family was well off, he hadn't given that much thought.

In the years when Hugh Mulzac was growing up, white and black attended the same churches, swam at the same beaches, studied at the same schools, sang *God Save the Queen*, or danced the *bongay* to the beat of African drums with equal fervor.

There were many things wrong with life in the British Island colonies in the early years of the twentieth century, but discrimination because of ancestry and color wasn't one of them. If Hugh Mulzac had been born in a mud hut on his father's plantation, he would probably never have gotten his hands on the big geography books that stirred his ambition to see the great world beyond the Caribbean Sea. He would scarcely have heard of Europe or the United States and the other countries of the American continents and would never have learned to read at all, for schooling was not free. His was a privileged position. Even so, he had worked along with his neighbors, helping milk the cows, taking his turn on the fishing boats. But he had all the time in the world to consider what he wanted to do with his future.

The world, as it unfolded before him in his school books, was his to explore. He took for granted that the vast seas, the continents beyond the confines of his small island, were open to any boy if he were willing to work hard. He knew neither the hardships of poverty nor the brutal and artificial hardships of prejudice and bigotry. To become captain of a barque or a schooner such as occasionally came in St. Vincent's harbor was, for Hugh Mulzac, not a vague dream, but a definite goal.

A first step was to sail, to learn to handle the lines, to steer the craft his older brothers used going from island to island on the family business. Then he would get a berth on an ocean liner. After that, only a few easy steps intervened in the boy's mind before "Captain Hugh Mulzac" would stand on the bridge of a four-master. He would sail across the ocean and home from the great world outside, in his blue serge uniform with brass buttons. He would carry a fortune in his pockets and presents from London, from New York, from the Orient; presents for his mother and sisters and for Edith, the lively, black-eyed girl he'd met at a church social in St. Vincent. Hugh Mulzac's was a fiercely personal ambition compounded of school-book learning and great confidence in his own capacities. His plan was his very own.

The second step, after he had sailed with his brother John for a few months on the schooner *Sunbeam,* was to get on a ship that was going somewhere away from the islands. His chance had come suddenly when the *Sunbeam* docked in the berth next to the *Aeolus* in the harbor of the large island of Barbados.

Captain Granderson's cargo was aboard. He was about to sail away from the port, but he was short an ordinary seaman. He walked down the gangplank and offered to sign on the eager, intelligent-looking West Indian who was staring up at the ship from the dock.

Young Hugh lost little time winning his brother John's

permission to sign the ship's articles for a voyage to London, with a stop in the States to pick up additional cargo. The fact that he would be the only Negro in the crew was of significance neither to himself nor to Captain Granderson.

The voyage to Wilmington had been an easy one, with clear weather and a crew of old-timers—mostly Danes, Norwegians, and Swedes—who cared nothing about the color of a man's skin. Captain Granderson, a Norwegian and part-time missionary, was pleased to have a seaman who had been brought up with proper religious training. Too many sailors, he said, were little better than infidels.

Nothing had prepared Hugh Mulzac for the incident at the church. It was a shattering blow. He never left the ship again all the time they were taking on cargo in Wilmington. He sat brooding in his bunk in the forecastle and writing letters home about the barbarous custom called segregation. Custom? Worse than that. It was a *law*. What if the whole outside world proved to be like Wilmington, North Carolina? He felt his dreams of the future slipping away; his self-confidence oozed from him like blood from a wound. He would have gone back home if his pride had let him. But he had signed on for London. In the English stories he'd read in his school library, a sailor never deserted his ship.

The voyage to London across the Atlantic took fifty days of struggle with wind and wave. Mountains of water attacked the ship and crashed over the bulwark. Somewhere along the way, battling with the elements, Hugh Mulzac's confidence came back to him and, with it, his confidence in his ability as a sailor, his great love of the sea, his dream of commanding a ship of his own.

He could have signed on again with Captain Granderson, but he wanted to see the sights of London. So, he took his pay and spent most of it on a set of navigation books and an engagement ring to send Edith. His money almost gone, he looked for another ship to sail on. The best he could do was a steamer bound for the Mediterranean.

For two years, Hugh Mulzac moved from ship to ship, from port to port—all the fascinating places that had been only names in geography books. Sometimes he signed on a barque or schooner, more often (for sailing ships were going out of fashion), on a dirty tramp steamer. Coal for Malta, grain for Russia or Constantinople, to the Argentine for logs to carry to Germany. Through Cape Horn to Australia.

Nowhere else, except in Australia, did he meet with the problem of the color bar. In Australia, however, it was worse than North Carolina. He was not even allowed to land and walk on the streets until the ship's captain put up bond. Again, he had met up with a law segregating colored men. But, this time, he had company in his misery. There were three others caught in the same humiliating situation, each from a different British colony: a Chinese seaman from Hong Kong, an Indian from Bombay, and a Jamaican.

"Who do they think they are—these Caucasians?" the sailor from Bombay said bitterly. "Don't they know we coloreds outnumber them in the world three to one?"

This idea was new to Hugh Mulzac, but was at the time,

small comfort. Segregation was still, to him, a personal insult, a hated obstacle to his own goal in life.

He was still a common seaman. Often captains were brutal to the men, often the food aboard ship was very bad, often he had to pay a "crimp" in port to get a berth on a ship. Never did he save any money. And his study of navigation from books alone went slowly.

He had learned that there were other obstacles than color to becoming a captain, but they were obstacles any sailor met with.

The next time he put into his home port of England, he took time off to go to Swansea Nautical College and passed the examination for his license as a second mate. Second mate was not like being a captain, but in his officer's uniform on the night watches, he began to think of going home to Edith.

Three voyages as an officer and he had saved forty pounds! He bought presents for all the family and sailed on the first ship he could get for Jamaica, one of the largest islands in the West Indies.

Hugh Mulzac never did get home. He waited thirteen days for a small inter-island boat going to Union Island. Before it came, his forty pounds had been stolen from his hotel room. Pride kept him from going home penniless. He signed on a British banana boat, plying its trade between the West Indies and Baltimore.

"Three more trips as second mate," he said to himself, "and I'll have my forty pounds again."

But the banana boat did not make three trips. At Baltimore, it went into dry dock for repairs. Second mate Mulzac was paid off with the rest. He found himself jobless in the land of segregation. The other officers were white and found new berths at once. But second mate Mulzac went from pier to pier looking for a job. The shipping clerks seemed to think it an affront for anyone of African descent to look for a deck job. "We hire 'niggers' for stewards and cooks." After this, Hugh did not even hint that he carried a certificate as an officer.

The year was 1911. Jobs at sea, even in the galley, were scarce. Hugh felt lucky, at last, to be taken on as second cook on a passenger cruiser.

He had never so much as boiled an egg in his life! He learned that job as he had learned navigation—from books. After some disasters, he became a good cook. But it was a long way from a cook's white cap to that blue serge captain's uniform.

Hugh Mulzac's bride-to-be evidently thought so. When he returned to Baltimore from one of his voyages, he had a letter from home informing him that Edith had married someone else. Suddenly, in 1913, Hugh Mulzac gave up and turned his back on the sea which he had so greatly loved.

For a year, he cooked in a fashionable girls' school outside Chicago. He found the life in a big city interesting and, for the first time, he met American Negroes and learned of their long history of struggle. He took out his first citizenship papers and put the easy life in the English island colonies behind him, as firmly as he had abandoned the sea.

However, in 1914, when the war broke out between France and England and Germany, he found that forgetting his past was not easy. Unlike many of his Negro American friends, he was swept up in the public indignation against the attacks on the Atlantic of the German submarines. He read in the daily papers how ships carrying war goods to England were being sunk in mid-ocean by U-boats. Surely, even with a black skin, a man who knew navigation could be of service!

He resigned his job at the girls' school and went back to Baltimore. He was right in thinking that there was a shortage of experienced seamen. After some difficulty, and the usual insults, he was assigned as second mate on a British ship going with a military convoy across the ocean to France. On the return trip, he was promoted to chief mate.

In 1917, when the United States entered World War I, Hugh Mulzac, now first mate, had been dodging submarines from the bridge of cargo ships for more than three years. He had begun to dream his old dream. But instead of a vision of himself as captain of a romantic sailing vessel, he dreamed of being in command of a twin-screw steamer in the service of his adopted country, after peace had been won. In spite of all its dangers, he loved every minute spent at sea.

With the tremendous energy of the American war effort, victory came with surprising speed. "A *war to end war. A war to make the world safe for democracy.*" Mulzac was carried away with the fine words in the papers and on the radio. He was proud to be an American. If he had been on shore more often, he might have become aware that the Negro people were far from sharing in President Wilson's high hopes; might have been prepared for what happened to him when the fighting was over.

After the Armistice was signed, Mulzac returned to Baltimore in high spirits. He knew he had been useful to the country in time of war. Now he would man its cargo ships in peace.

He married a young Baltimore woman, his landlady's daughter. But this marriage was not a happy one. They were divorced after a very bad few years; he was awarded custody of their one child, Elaine.

He took the examination for his master's license and passed with a perfect paper, having finished the test in seven hours—a record time. His picture appeared in the *Baltimore Sun:* "The first colored seaman to win a master's certificate!" But he found no job as captain.

As a first mate, he made one peacetime voyage, to Finland. When his ship returned to port in New York, the crew and the officers were paid off and told that their vessel would not be put into service again. First mate Mulzac hurried to Baltimore to register for a new assignment. He applied for membership in the Masters, Mates, and Pilots Union and received the first hint of what was to come. A clause in the union's constitution prohibited Negroes from becoming members.

The war had changed nothing!

On the high seas, in wartime, it had been different. Danger and death knew no color bars. Maybe it could be different still. Doggedly, Mulzac sat in the United States Shipping Board Office where berths on outgoing ships were assigned. He sat there and waited while other men, with less experience than he had, were assigned to ships— if their skin was white.

Finally he protested. "Look here, I've been sitting for two months with a master's certificate. I've watched you give assignments to men with temporary red-ink second mate's licenses. What's the idea?"

The answer was blunt and clear. "Look here, buddy, as long as there's a white man in this hall, you'll never ship out of here."

Returning soldiers and sailors were receiving the same kind of treatment—or worse. Negro men and women who had worked on the home front were being thrown out of jobs they had held to make the way for white workers. Lynchings in the deep South were reported without comment and without punishment. Riots had broken out— one of the most serious in the capital itself. It is no wonder that thousands of oppressed colored people over the nation were listening to Marcus Garvey's cry of "Back to Africa" as to a Promised Land.

"The Back to Africa Movement? Haven't you heard about it? No, it's nothing to do with Dr. Du Bois' Pan African Congress. This is practical dollars and cents. It's the greatest thing that's happened to us in years," a ship's cook from Mississippi said. "A fellow in New York is organizing it—name of Marcus Garvey. We're going to have our own business, own factories, our own steamship company. The *Black Star Line*. They're advertising for colored officers."

A week later, Hugh Mulzac was ushered into Mr. Garvey's office at the "Universal Negro Improvement Association."

A short, stocky man with deep black eyes and skin the color of ebony came from behind his desk. "Glad to see you, Captain Mulzac, sit down, sit down."

Like Mulzac, Marcus Garvey was a West Indian. His plan for a unity of people of African descent with those on the African continent had its beginning in Jamaica.

"The whites practice segregation. Very well," Garvey had said, "the Negro will segregate *himself*."

Money was pouring into the movement—the small savings of a million disfranchised, ignored, forgotten Afro-Americans. They had begun to feel a pride in the history of their ancestors whom Du Bois, in the *Crisis*, wrote about over and over again. A few had been caught up in the spell of the poetry of young Countee Cullen:

What is Africa to me:
Copper sun or scarlet sea,
Jungle star or jungle track,
Strong bronze men, or regal black
Women from whose loins I sprang
When the birds of Eden sang?

One three centuries removed
From the scenes his fathers loved,
Spicy grove, cinnamon tree,
What is Africa to me?

They became vaguely aware of Pan-African Congresses where American Negroes met yearly with Negroes from the African colonies and talked Freedom. Hugh Mulzac had not thought of himself as an *Afro*-American. He had received his citizenship papers during the war with pride in being American, the equal of any other citizen in this great country. But he had not been treated as an equal. Now this fellow West Indian was going to give him a chance to show what he could do. He was carried along on Garvey's enthusiasm, and happily accepted an offer to become chief mate on the first ship of the *Black Star Line*. A captaincy seemed not far away.

It did not take Mulzac long to see that Garvey's grandiose dreams were castles in the air. The great fleet of vessels the man talked of so glibly consisted of two excursion boats and one twenty-four-year-old steamship flying the British flag, and captained by a British African—a capable man, but not a magician. And only a magician could have carried on a profitable trade under the many handicaps. Mulzac was disappointed, but not surprised when the *Black Star Line* and all of Marcus Garvey's business enterprises collapsed in 1922.

"For a few brief years," he wrote years later, "Marcus Garvey fired the torch that lighted the Negro night, bringing dreams of glory and equality. Just as quickly, the torch flickered and was out, leaving us in darkness as before."

The next years were bad for Hugh Mulzac, but into the bleak picture had come a ray of wisdom. All this while, since boyhood, his struggle for a place in the world had been just for himself. Every setback, every act of discrimination he had suffered seemed directed at him alone. To fulfill his ambition had been all that had mattered. It had not taken him long to understand that, in a world controlled by whites, the principal obstacle was his color. But every failure, every small triumph was for himself alone. His crusade was personal. Then, suddenly, like sunlight breaking through fog on the horizon, he realized that no one can wage a battle against injustice and discrimination as a single individual.

"For too long," he wrote, "I fought my lonely battle for recognition with one arm tied behind my back. The fight is the fight not only of the colored races, but of poor working people, black or white."

Even before the 1929 depression, thousands of broken, dispirited veterans of World War I roamed the waterfront in search of jobs. There was no central hiring hall; the hours of work on ships were increased from fifty-six hours a week to eighty-four; wages dropped.

In 1920, Hugh Mulzac married a second time, to Miriam Aris, a Jamaican girl he had known for a long time. Together, they had made plans for the home he'd come back to after every voyage. He now had a family to support— a wife and three much-loved daughters.

There was nothing to do but go to sea as a ship's cook. In the years from 1925 to 1942, there was not one Negro officer in the entire U.S. Merchant Marine. The steamship companies reduced wages and lengthened hours of work still further as the depression deepened. Suddenly, on both the East Coast and the West, sailors and longshoremen began to talk of organizing unions. Mulzac threw himself into the movement.

Marine workers' "Industrial Clubs" had come into action in almost every port. In 1933, just before Franklin Delano Roosevelt took office as President of the United States, delegates met and voted to form a union with membership open to all "without discrimination because of race, creed, or color."

Forming a union to make demands for decent working conditions was just a beginning. It took years, it took long strikes, it took lives, it took the weight of new laws and changed thinking on the part of the American people for the Maritime Unions to win contracts from the owners of ships that put out to sea. The 1930's had almost come to a close before the unions of common seamen, stewards, and longshoremen could be said to have won the right for their members, Negro or white, to bargain for some control over their conditions of labor.

When war broke out among the European nations again, Hugh Mulzac was still working in the ship's galleys as a steward. The Masters, Mates, and Pilots Union had not changed its rules for membership. There were still only white officers on the bridge of American ships. In the galley of a luxury liner, Hugh had made three trips around the world. He had seen, in hundreds of ports on four continents, the appalling difference between the poorer, darker peoples and their white overlords.

"Somehow," he said to his fellow crew members, referring to the German and Italian atrocities, "somehow, white people have got to be made to realize that Negroes, even in our own country, have suffered the same terrors all their lives."

America was slowly being drawn into the war on the side of Great Britain and her allied forces. Under Roosevelt's leadship, there was a strong chance that the Negro American's long history of suffering could be changed. The war could be fought with success only if it was fought as a *democratic* struggle. This was the meaning of the President's Four Freedoms—freedom to speak, freedom of religion, freedom from want, freedom from fear. It was the meaning of Philip Randolph's March on Washington Movement that had won equality in jobs for hundreds of thousands.

"But what of my own role in this struggle?" Hugh Mulzac asked himself.

He had been at sea for thirty-five years, had passed every

examination of seamanship, and still had to sail as either a cook or steward. And his case was not unique. He was acquainted with several other men who had carried unused master's certificates in their wallets for years. What if *he* could break the color bar in the Navy or Merchant Marine? Would that not be a service as useful as that of the soldiers now pleading in Washington for unsegregated officers' training camps? Or the young men trying to be accepted for training in the Air Force?

"The President himself has demanded the full mobilization of manpower. We don't need training," Hugh said to himself. "All we need is a chance."

Mulzac asked for the help of various civil rights organizations and met only with frustration. The rebuffs hurt, but Mulzac was no longer concerned with his personal ambition. His country was at war, and he had a right to serve to the best of his abilities. He persisted against all advice of union officials and the NAACP.

"You'll never make it," friends in the union said sadly. "They're not going to give a colored man command of a ship."

At last, Captain Edward McCauley of the War Shipping Board consented to give Hugh Mulzac an interview. Mulzac came prepared. He placed a portfolio of advertisements he had clipped from newspapers appealing for experienced seafaring men for the Merchant Marine on the captain's desk.

"I came to answer these ads in person," he said. "I am a United States citizen and have a held a master's license since 1918. In the past twenty-four years, I have never been able to sail on it. Here is my license. Here are two diplomas in ocean navigation. Here are my discharges as a chief mate in World War I. The country needs Merchant Marine officers and here I am."

The white officer looked at the tall, heavy-built, serious-eyed man standing before him. His own eyes dropped. "This is plainly a case of discrimination," he said slowly.

"Of segregation," Mulzac murmured, and stared at a photograph of the President in Navy uniform and a poster on the opposite wall expounding the Four Freedoms: *freedom of speech, freedom of religion, freedom from want, freedom from fear.*

"Excuse me a moment," McCauley said and picked up the portfolio and the license and diplomas and left the room.

Mulzac waited a half hour, not daring to look ahead with hope, unwilling to look back at the past. Finally, Captain McCauley returned, beaming.

Here, in Mulzac's words is what happened next:

" 'Captain Mulzac,' McCauley said firmly, 'it has been decided to name a ship, now in a California shipyard, the Booker T. Washington. We are asking Miss Marian Anderson to christen her. And Captain, we think you would fit in just perfectly as master of the Booker T.'

"Captain McCauley raised his eyes to mine and his face fell as he saw the look of confused joy and dismay that must have been reflected in my features. How could I explain the bitter and cruel irony of his offer! The American Revolution had been fought in 1776, and a Constitution written guaranteeing equality for all. A Civil War had been fought eighty-three years earlier over the same issue of freedom for colored citizens. And here we were, in 1942, engaged in the greatest war in history, in which one of the major issues was the ruthless extermination of a minority people, and demanding the fullest mobilization of the nation's manpower. If there was ever a moment when the real meaning of democracy could and had to be demonstrated to the peoples of the world, the moment was now! And what was America's answer in this hour of need? A Jim Crow ship! Named for a Negro, christened by a Negro, captained by a Negro, and no doubt manned by Negroes!

"Captain McCauley, for possibly the noblest of reasons, was preparing to launch a segregated liberty ship in the very name of democracy! There wasn't a colored citizen anywhere in the world who would fail to recognize such an act as evidence of discrimination in America.

" 'Captain, I appreciate your good will and your offer. And let me say that I can get enough colored sailors to man one ship, five ships, or ten ships. But it would, in my opinion, be wrong, for they would be Jim Crow ships. That's what we're fighting against. And for me to lend my name to such a project would be wrong.'

" 'I don't understand,' Captain McCauley said. 'You said you wanted a ship and now I'm offering one to you and you turn it down. What do you want us to do? Do you expect that white men will sail under you?'

" 'Captain McCauley, I can get an entire crew of white sailors, too, if need be, but that would be just as wrong. I think we should get crew members without any regard to their color. Do you ask white captains to get all-white crews? Of course not! The union would forbid it. What we should do is put in a call to the union hall for a crew, white or black. I cannot accept the appointment on the terms you are offering me. Give me an appointment the same as you would any other man.' "

This is finally what came about. Captain Hugh Mulzac received the assignment and went to the National Maritime Union hiring hall in San Pedro, California, to get a crew. White members of the union had called a special meeting. On a motion unanimously passed, the union membership voted to suspend shipping rules on the grounds that it was a signal honor to sail on the *Booker T.* and that the privilege should go to the most experienced men available!

Captain Mulzac of the *Booker T. Washington* sailed out of the San Pedro harbor on the 23rd of October, 1942, with a crew that read like the United Nations—two Danes, a Turk, five Filipinos, a British Guianan, a Norwegian, a Belgian, two British West Indians, a Honduran, and sailors, white and Negro, from thirteen different states of the Union.

Furthermore, remembering Captain McCauley's remark that white men would not sail under Negro officers, Mulzac decided for the first voyage to choose both of his top officers from among qualified Negro Americans. The chief mate was Adolphus Folks and the second mate was Clifton Lastic. Hugh Mulzac had trained both of these men in the art of navigation in the days of the *Black Star* experiment.

Lastic, unable to get on a ship, was working on a tugboat in New York's harbor when Mulzac sought him out. Folks had quit the sea entirely and was working ashore.

"Captain, I see you got yourself a big job!" he had said when Mulzac appeared at his home.

"And you've got yourself a big job, too," Captain Mulzac answered. "You're the chief mate of the *Booker T.*"

Now, as the *Booker T.* put out to sea, the three officers stood for a moment on the deck of their ship, together, watching the pilot go over the side. At last, Hugh Mulzac was master of his own ship, with forty-two sailors under his command and faithful friends for mates at his side. And 10,000 tons of cargo were entrusted to him in a cause worth fighting for.

"This is everything," he said in a choked voice. And he meant everything he had dreamed of, trained for, struggled for, for nearly half a century.

With his ship out of the harbor and pointed toward the open sea, Captain Hugh Mulzac gave the command that the engine room—and freedom—had been waiting for: "Full speed ahead!"

The history of the *Booker T. Washington* in the Second World War was such that people still speak of it proudly today. She was a Liberty Ship in more ways than one. From 1942 to the moment of victory in 1945, Captain Mulzac and his crew brought thousands of tons of war supplies to England, to the African Coast at Casablanca, to the Russian ports in the Baltic, under actual fire to Italy, and finally, to a liberated France. On return trips to the home port of New York, the *Booker T.* brought prisoners of war—Italians and Germans. When the war was over, she became a transport to bring American soldiers back to their homes.

The officers and the members of the crew changed from time to time. Always the personnel was interracial. Always the members of the crew gave the best that was in them to win the struggle against an enemy that believed one race should be the master over all others. The officers and

the crew members under Hugh Mulzac were true "freedom fighters." With the confidence gained through the long, slow experience, Captain Mulzac was able to imbue them with faith in the future and with the real meaning of our country's heritage.

Out of the wisdom won through his own struggle, Hugh Mulzac came to know who and what he was. To the question, "Who am I?" he answered: "I am a man, as other men, not alone but a part of the people of the world, fighting the common battle of all people for a life of freedom and plenty."

And yet at the end of his life, Hugh Mulzac suffered the great loneliness and frustration of a man who saw the victory he had helped to win brought down again to defeat.

When the last voyage of the Liberty Ship *Booker T. Washington* was completed, Mulzac was compelled to spend many months in a veteran's hospital, his health shattered by the long strain of war.

In 1946, when he was discharged from the hospital, he had to admit that he was an old man—old and homeless, for his wife had died during his absence. His children were grown. Yet, restored to health, Hugh Mulzac felt that he had some years of usefulness ahead. His long experience at sea was surely an asset. He reported for duty.

But, with the ending of the war, the climate of opinion in America had changed. The Fair Employment Practices Committee (F.E.P.C.) had gone out of existence. President Roosevelt's Executive Order 8802 had been a war measure. Roosevelt was dead. The men he had drawn to his side in Washington had been replaced. The new Congress, led by Southern segregationists, refused to create a permanent F.E.P.C. Negro American officers aboard ships were no longer needed—not while white Americans were waiting in hiring halls for jobs. "Last hired, first fired" was once again the fate of men with dark skins.

To make things even more difficult, the "cold war" was gathering its forces to undermine the unity of peoples in the world and to set American against American. In the United States Senate, Joseph McCarthy of Wisconsin had begun to stir suspicion against people who had spoken out freely for Franklin Delano Roosevelt's Four Freedoms. "McCarthyism" extended even as far as the relatively obscure Captain Hugh Mulzac, and he was blacklisted along with hundreds of others as "subversive."

For months and years, Hugh Mulzac fought a losing fight for command of another ship on the high seas. His age was against him, too, and neither he nor the other Negro officers who had trained under him ever rose again to a captaincy of a seagoing vessel. Like the ships they had sailed, they were put in dry dock in the New York Harbor.

Mulzac finished out the last few years of his life as "night-mate" in the lonely hours aboard ships. And in the days, in a seaman's boarding house, he worked on his autobiography, A Star to Steer By, putting down for the future the story of one man in the struggle to "let America be America." He realized that, on the S.S. Booker T. Washington, he had won only a single battle against segregation. Others would have to go on without him to win the war.

4 / *Hammer of Justice*

I've got a hammer,
I've got a bell,
I've got a song to sing
All over this land.
It's the hammer of justice,
It's the bell of freedom,
It's the song of love
Between my brothers and sisters
All over this land.

LEE HAYS AND PETE SEEGER / *If I Had a Hammer**

A handful of American citizens, men and women, white and non-white, meeting together in 1910 to found the National Association for the Advancement of Colored

* *If I Had a Hammer (The Hammer Song); Words and music by Lee Hays and Pete Seeger; © Copyright 1958 and 1962 Ludlow Music, Inc., New York, N.Y.; Used by permission.*

People announced their goals. Fifty-three years later, in 1963, two hundred and fifty thousand people poured into the nation's capital to march for these same still unfulfilled goals. In the spring of 1965, many of those same Americans were on an Alabama road, marching once more under the needed protection of Federal troops, witnesses to the fact that full freedom was not yet won. The signs they carried, the songs they sang, made the same demands put forward by the little group who founded the NAACP in 1910: abolition of enforced segregation, equal advantages for colored and white, enfranchisement for the Negro, and enforcement of the Fourteenth and Fifteenth Amendments to the Constitution of the United States.

The enforcement of the Constitutional Amendments, then as now, encompassed all the rest. The American Constitution is, in many ways, a unique instrument of government. It is the oldest written constitution in operation in the world, the first to recognize the right of a people to govern themselves." We, the People . . . ." The strong, clear words of the preamble, together with the first ten amendments, which we call the Bill of Rights, and the Thirteenth and Fourteenth and Fifteenth Amendments, abolishing slavery, guaranteeing equal protection of the law for all citizens and the right to vote "without regard to race or creed," are designed to insure freedom. Yet freedom for ten million dark-skinned Americans is denied. The difficulty lies in the enforcement of that promise made so long ago and at such cost in lives and suffering.

The Congress and the legislative branch of the several states are empowered to make laws, the executive branch to see that the laws are enforced—provided that they are in agreement with the principles of the Constitution and its amendments. This is left to the Supreme Court of the Federal government to decide.

The only way in which the Supreme Court can be called on to declare a law unconstitutional, whether it is a law passed by Congress or by a state legislature, is on the complaint of an individual citizen. A case can only be brought to the Supreme Court after the facts have been argued in lower courts. The Supreme Court then decides whether the rights guaranteed to the individual under the Constitution have been abused or violated. The method is slow and cumbersome and expensive, and the interpretation of the judges—the protectors of Constitutional rights—depends on many factors, including the climate of opinion and the conditions at the time. Judges are human beings. They do not live in a vacuum.

Occasionally, the decisions they make have been disastrous. In the case of the Negro, Dred Scott, he was returned from a free state to slavery because five Southern-born Supreme Court judges, in 1857, believed that Negroes were property and not citizens with rights protected by the Constitution. That decision was instrumental in bringing on the Civil War. In 1896, the decision known as "Plessy vs. Ferguson" ruled "separate but equal" accommodations on a railroad train satisfied the constitutional guarantees of the Fourteenth Amendment. That decision opened the door to *legal* segregation in everything—the hospital a child was born in, his home, his school, his work.

As Louis Lomax explained, that 1896 decision meant a Negro in the South was Jim-Crowed "from the day he was born until he was carried to a Jim Crow cemetery to be buried.

But faulty interpretations of the Constitution can be

overturned, and this is exactly what the NAACP set out to do. Its purpose was to change the conditions of life for ten million Americans deprived of equal protection under the Constitution. The method the NAACP relied on most strongly was the courts. Between 1915 and 1938, the NAACP legal department won many small victories. With each court decision in its favor, Southerners of African descent, men and women who had been *almost* crushed into submissiveness, were heartened, and the climate of public opinion in the whole country began to change. The slow, cumbersome, and expensive struggle in the courts continued. To the courageous private citizens who were willing to bring suit against abuses, and to devoted staff of lawyers in the Legal Defense and Education Fund—lawyers such as William Hastie, Charles Houston, and young Thurgood Marshall—belongs the credit for laying a foundation for the "second American Revolution" that is going on today.

Thurgood Marshall

In the summer of 1938, a husky, black-haired, tan-skinned young man leaned back in his swivel chair and sighed. The lettering on the open office door read *Thurgood Marshall, Attorney at Law*. There was nothing impressive about the office, a weather-beaten room in a run-down building in Baltimore, Maryland. The rent was cheap and, in the five years he'd been practicing, Marshall had found it adequate. His eyes took in the desk piled high with papers.

It wasn't that he didn't have plenty of work. But his cases—bringing suit against landlords who were too quick with evictions, acting as local representative for the NAACP on a few civil rights cases in the state courts before they were passed on for appeal, getting Negro boys out of trouble with the white police—didn't bring in much money, hardly as much as he had made as a bellhop or dining-car waiter when he was working his way through Lincoln University.

"You would think that after four years at college and three at Howard Law School, the busiest lawyer in Maryland could earn enough to pay the office rent," he said to himself.

There was some satisfaction, of course, in representing people who otherwise would have no lawyer at all, especially the so-called delinquent boys. He could understand how their high spirits and aimless existence got them into mischief. They reminded him of the gang he had liked to play ball with as a boy. He chuckled, thinking of those times. His family had always been pretty well off. With his father working as steward out at the white country club and his mother teaching, they could afford to live in a nice, mixed neighborhood, white neighbors on each side. His brothers played with the neighbors' sons, but he had always preferred the kids on the street facing their back yard. The old rickety houses back there were rented mostly by Negro families from the South, with swarms of children, dead poor and a little wild.

"When it was dinnertime," his mother used to explain, "I'd go to the front door to call the rest of the children, but Thurgood, I'd have to call from the back yard."

Well, he was still a back yard boy, only kids like those were now his clients. Plenty of work for a Negro practicing law in Baltimore, where there was an average of one Negro lawyer for ten thousand possible clients. Once in a while, too, a white storekeeper would come in to have installment papers fixed up. At least, it wasn't Mississippi where he had heard the ratio was one to 168,000, and enough local laws on the books to put a Negro on a chain gang any time a policeman took a notion!

Thurgood Marshall took his feet off the desk and pulled a batch of papers toward him, knocking over his wife's picture in the process. He felt a twinge of regret for her sake that success was coming so slowly. They had married while he was still in law school, with everybody predicting such great things ahead when he graduated *summa cum laude*. They would just have to go along with things as they were until he had built up a paying practice.

The phone rang. "Long distance. New York calling."

William Hastie's familiar voice came through the receiver. Judge Hastie. Until he had been appointed Governor of the Virgin Islands, he had been with Charles Houston, the mainstay of the NAACP Legal Department. Now, President Roosevelt had appointed Hastie a Circuit Court Judge, the highest any Negro had gone in the judiciary.

"How's Your Honor?" Marshall asked jovially. Both Houston and Hastie had been his teachers at Howard.

Judge Hastie went right to the point. "I'm in the NAACP office, Thurgood," he said. "Houston and the legal department are swamped. We were wondering if you'd like to come on the staff."

"Your appointment made us all pretty proud."

"Thanks," Hastie interrupted. "About this other thing, your record at law school is still tops, Thurgood. In the five years you've been out, nobody's matched it, especially in Constitutional Law. That's the key to our work. It would mean closing your office, of course, giving up your practice."

Thurgood Marshall was thinking fast. Taking a job with the NAACP would mean leaving Baltimore where he and his wife had lived all their lives, where his whole family lived. As a staff man in the legal defense department, he would have to travel in the states of the deep South—an area which, up to now, he had carefully avoided.

"There are big things coming up," Hastie urged. "Houston has plans to crack the whole segregation picture right down the middle—but I'll let him tell you when you get here."

"You're twisting my arm," the younger man said with a laugh.

"Maybe I am, but we need you. Think it over. Talk to the family. Call me back when you decide."

Thurgood Marshall had been in the office on West 40th Street in New York for a month when the fall term of the Supreme Court was due to open. He had been working directly with Charles Houston on the case of *Gaines Versus the State of Missouri*. Young Gaines wanted to study law. And he wanted to get his training, not in an Eastern law school, not even as far from his home as Howard in Washington, D.C., but right in his home state of Missouri. There he meant to practice, there he paid his taxes, there any student could go if his grades were good—and his skin were white. But Gaines was a Negro and the University, segregated by state law, had refused to admit him. The state had no law school for Negroes, and Gaines had called on the NAACP for assistance.

The legal department reasoned that this was a clear case of discrimination. Not even the old ruling of separate but equal educational facilities could be given as an excuse. Graduate training in the professions was not available to a Negro in Missouri. The NAACP had carried the suit through all the lower courts and now was going to the Supreme Court in Washington. The Court had agreed last year, in 1937, to hear the arguments because a question of Constitutional rights was raised. The case had been put on the calendar for the coming session.

The arguments had been carefully prepared. Houston had searched out every decision in the history of the Court to bolster his position that Gaines had been denied rights guaranteed under the Fourteenth Amendment. Marshall, fascinated, had stayed up late every night checking the citations. Now Charles Houston was ready to appear before the nine justices in the nation's capital.

On the night before the presentation, Houston said, "I thought you might want to come along, Thurgood. I ordered two Pullman tickets."

In the years when he was studying at Howard, Thurgood Marshall had passed by the white-columned Supreme Court building hundreds of times. Many times, he had stared up at the massive oak door and thought, "In there are the protectors of our civil rights." (It was only at Howard that he had come to understand that he *had* any civil rights.) But he had never stepped inside the impressive halls.

The first thing that he noticed, as he followed Charles Houston through the door, was the noble simplicity of the high-ceilinged corridors. In his mind came a picture of a vast overpowering courtroom. Then, a page opened a door to a simple, wood-paneled room, not as large as many police courtrooms he had been in. There was, of course, no witness stand, no railed-off jury box. There were just a few comfortable chairs ranged along the side walls and, at the end of the room, a low, semi-circular table with nine arm chairs placed behind it. When a small door was quietly opened in the back wall, nine robed men—plain ordinary men—walked in and sat down. In their persons was all the "majesty of the law" his teachers had talked about.

As had happened to so many other young lawyers, Thurgood Marshall succumbed to "love at first sight." He caught his breath to think that he was really here; an observer today, but perhaps someday a participant in the proceedings which could set a precedent and change the lives of thousands. Suppose he had not accepted Hastie's offer!

Copies of the brief that he had helped prepare were on the table before each of the judges—and the brief of Houston's opponent, the thin, wiry, blond Missourian across the room. After the arguments of the two lawyers, the justices asked a few low-toned, informal questions, and the presentation of *Gaines Versus the State of Missouri* was over. No one knew just when the decision would be handed down. It might be in a few weeks. It might not come until the end of the term.

"We'll win," Charles Houston declared on the train carrying them back to New York. "It's just a beginning. There has been a slow but steady progression in the decisions of the court to enforce the equal protection by the law to all citizens. That doesn't mean that they've abandoned the 'separate but equal' doctrine—not yet. But

Missouri will have to open a second law school just for one Negro, if they want to keep their precious segregation. If the taxpayers object to the extra expense, maybe they'll cut through their Jim Crow nonsense and say to Gaines, 'Come on in. Study with the whites.' Either way, we will have knocked a few bricks out of the segregation wall."

"And the walls will come tumblin' down?" Thurgood Marshall's eyes were sparkling.

Houston nodded. "That's my idea. Begin with the graduate schools, let 'em see that the black doesn't come off on the law books. Eventually, you'll see integrated colleges in the deep South as well as in border states like Missouri. From colleges, we'll work down through the high schools, insisting on equal education—even if it's separate. Then to elementary schools. Suit after suit for equal education, equal money for buildings and equipment. Equal courses taught by teachers paid equally."

"That would take a bite out of the tax dollar, wouldn't it? I understand in the deep South they pay ten dollars for educating a white child to every two dollars spent on a child in a Negro school."

"Exactly," Houston went on. "And then they look at education-starved boys and girls and say, 'You see, they're not as good as our children. It's just too bad, but they're an inferior race.' As Mrs. Bethune says, 'We live in a vicious circle.' When the white Southerners begin to complain about the cost of two expensive school systems, we'll go further. Meanwhile, we put our social science professors to work—not just Negroes, but those whites who are on our side. Let them prove what we already know to be true, that separate can never be equal, that segregation doesn't belong in a democratic society, and that the doctrine hasn't any place in our constitutional law."

"What a dream picture!" Marshall sighed. "Pretty daring isn't it?"

"Daring, yes. Impossible, no. We can't stop where we are. What I intend is nothing less than a change in the interpretation the court puts on the Fourteenth Amendment—roll back the law to the original intention of wiping out all legal distinction between black and white."

"I had no idea—" Thurgood Marshall felt humble before the clarity of Houston's grand design.

"It will take years—maybe my whole lifetime, maybe yours or your kids'. But segregation in the schools has got to go. We've put our hands to the plow."

For the rest of that year, Thurgood Marshall was sent down to appear before state and federal courts in the South. He saw firsthand the need to change conditions. The poverty, the fear, the constant reminders that certain southerners were, merely because of the color of their skin, inferior. The fact that many of the Negro southerners had come to believe this themselves created in Marshall a burning anger and impatience to get on with the job.

However, lawyers in the legal department did not bring cases to court to suit their own desire. When requested by local chapters of the NAACP, they came to the assistance of Negroes whose rights as citizens were being abused. Many problems they dealt with had nothing to do with schools. And ten years passed after the 1938 decision in favor of Gaines of Missouri before another major civil rights case came before the Supreme Court involving equality of education.

In 1939, Thurgood Marshall was admitted to practice in the Supreme Court. The first case he and Houston tried together was an appeal from a case Marshall had lost in a Mississippi court—a Negro being tried for killing a white man, tried before an all-white jury. The trial was a farce. It occurred to Marshall that he could raise the question again before the Supreme Court of a violation of "due process of law" because no Negroes were on the lists from which the jury was drawn. A precedent had been set on this in 1935 in Oklahoma. The ruling of the Court in that case had been studiously ignored in the deep South. Marshall won a second trial for the accused, but the man did not live to stand trial again. He died in jail, whether by violence or because of sickness no one could ever be sure. Nevertheless, the case set a precedent in Mississippi. Thereafter, Negroes were called to jury duty in Mississippi and other Southern states. But only a token number. The wheels of justice grind slowly.

"You see how constitutional law *can* be changed," Houston said.

A few months later, just before the outbreak of World War II, Thurgood Marshall was put in charge of the whole staff of the department. Charles Houston remained as chairman, but he had decided to return to Washington to go into private practice with his father, who was too old to carry the load of work alone. During the war years, and for some time afterward, Thurgood Marshall fought for the rights of Negro Americans and won case after case in the Supreme Court. Because of his work, returned veterans had a slightly better chance than before to buy decent houses to live in, especially in the North and West, when Marshall succeeded in proving that the so-called "restrictive covenants" (a promise not to sell to Negroes or other dark-skinned people written into deeds), were against the Constitution. As a result of another case, those Negroes who were registered to vote in the Southern states were no longer denied a voice in the primaries.

But the only case that came up in these years that had to do with education was the question of equal pay for the Negro teachers. After a battle, Marshall won that case, too. Still, he and Charles Houston were no further ahead in the plan to integrate schools. More and more, Marshall came to believe that that was the heart of the problem. Then, in the late 1940's, two more graduate students, Sweatt of Texas and McLaurin of Oklahoma, tried to get training in law and were refused in the state universities. Again, the Supreme Court gave the verdict that the men must be given the equal opportunity for training within their states. Texas, bent on segregation, opened a law school of a sort just for one student. Oklahoma admitted McLaurin, but put him behind a screen and made him eat in the cafeteria at a different time from his white colleagues. In neither case could this be called "equal" educational opportunity. Marshall brought the cases back before the court and won. Both men were admitted on equal terms to their state universities. Hundreds of young men and women in the Southern states were able, through the precedent thus set, to get professional training. In a few states, undergraduate colleges began to integrate.

Thurgood Marshall had dinner with the Houstons in Washington to celebrate the victory.

"It's time to make the next move," Houston said. "Between us," the older man continued, "we'll carry out the job."

They proceeded then and there to outline plans for building the cases that would pull down segregation in high school and elementary school education. Thurgood Marshall left, filled with excitement at the prospect of working with Charles Houston again.

Six months later, before a start had been made, the dreamer, Charles Houston, was dead, unexpectedly, tragically. His illness and death came so suddenly, it was hard for Marshall to accept. On the shoulders of the younger man rested the whole responsibility for carrying out the older man's dream.

In the spring of 1951, Marshall had five elementary school cases in lower courts in various parts of the country. Parents of children in Virginia, Delaware, the District of Columbia, and South Carolina asked that suits be brought to have equal education provided for their children. The fifth case was brought by the Reverend Oliver Brown of Topeka, Kansas. His nine-year-old daughter, Linda, attended a segregated school that was, in every respect, equal to the elementary schools in Topeka provided for white pupils. But it was across town—and there was a school for white children just four blocks from their home.

Here was the chance Marshall had waited for. The Browns were suing to transfer their daughter to the neighborhood school for whites. Somewhere along the line through the lower courts, the parents in South Carolina changed their plea to match the Browns' of Topeka. They, too, asked for admission of their children to a white school. "To be truly equal, to be truly free, black and white children," they said, "ought to get their schooling together. Otherwise *both* races are underprivileged."

In 1953, with a whole staff of lawyers and experts, Marshall faced his opponent, John W. Davis of West Virginia, once a candidate for President. The court had said they would argue the constitutional question of all five cases together. The justices had read the briefs and now they listened to the arguments. The routine over the years had become as familiar to Thurgood Marshall as his impressive figure (he stood six feet tall and weighed two hundred pounds) was to members of the Court. But there was one justice in the courtroom to whom Marshall was a stranger —Chief Justice Earl Warren of California. Marshall worried a little about the impression he was making on the newly appointed judge, whose opinions were not clearly known. He could only hope, as he and his colleagues filed out of the courtroom.

Then came the period of waiting, while the nine men considered. The whole country was tense, Thurgood Marshall most of all. It seemed to him that his whole life's purpose was tied up in the decision the Court would make.

"Sometimes," he said, "the law has to lead the people. If we win, the whites in the South won't like it and yet it's as much for their good as for ours."

He remembered what Charles Houston had said so often: if they could desegregate the public schools of America, the whole pattern of racial segregation would eventually collapse. Would it happen on this round? Or would we have it all to do again?

May 15. May 16. The last weekend before the end of the Supreme Court term! The decision would have to come on the morrow. Marshall took a plane to Washington Sunday night. If he slept that night, it would be a miracle.

Monday, May 17, 1954, was the day of the Great Decision. Before a full courtroom of spectators, Chief Justice Warren read the Court's *unanimous* decision almost in the words Thurgood Marshall had used in his argument: "The Plaintiffs contend that segregated public schools are not equal and cannot be made equal and hence they, the children, are deprived of equal protection of the laws." Justice Warren read on in the silence of the courtroom. "Does segregation of children in public schools solely on the basis of race, even though the physical facilities and other factors may be equal, deprive children of the minority group of equal educational opportunities? We believe that it does. . . . To separate them (Negro children) from others of similar age and qualifications solely because of their race generates a feeling of inferiority as to their status in the community that may affect their hearts and minds in a way unlikely ever to be undone. . . ."

People all around Thurgood Marshall were wiping tears of joy from their eyes. He sat still as a statue, and listened to the voice of the Chief Justice roll on. "Therefore, we conclude that in the field of public education the doctrine of 'separate but equal' has no place. Separate education is inherently unequal. . . ."

Sooner than Charles Houston could have imagined, his dream was realized. The decision wouldn't bring heaven on earth, Marshall reminded himself, but it did lay a foundation for a new America.

The people in that courtroom were not alone in their rejoicing. The news was flashed by wire, by radio, by newspaper headlines over the world. Louis Lomax, then a boy still in a segregated Georgia school, remembers what the feeling among the Negro children was like.

This is the way Lomax described it: "The Supreme Court school desegregation decision was an electric thing, coming—as it most certainly did—just as the Negro was at the breaking point. . . . It would be impossible for a white person to understand what happened within black breasts on that Monday. An ardent segregationist has called it 'Black Monday.' He was so right, but for reasons other than the ones he advances: That was the day we won; the day we took the white man's law and won our case before an all-white Supreme Court with a Negro lawyer, Thurgood Marshall, as our chief counsel. And we were proud."

The effect of the May 17, 1954 decision was indeed electric. It sparked an explosion. The cases on which the decision of the Supreme Court was based were, because of "the wide applicability of the decision and because of the great variety of the local conditions," restored to the docket. The final decree was not handed down until May 31, 1955. On that date, the District Courts were ordered "to take such proceedings and enter such orders and decrees consistent with this (the Court's decision) as are necessary and proper to admit to public schools on a racially non-discriminatory basis with all deliberate speed. . . . It is so ordered."

The decision did not, as Marshall said, bring "heaven on earth," or even an end to injustice.

The order of the highest court of the land has, over ten years later, yet to be enforced for the vast majority of Negro school children in the Southern states. It has been estimated that at the rate desegregation has gone forward so far, full compliance will take about ninety-nine years.

For seven years more, Thurgood Marshall was in the

forefront of the never-ending, heartbreaking job. When President Kennedy, in 1961, appointed Marshall Judge of the Court of Appeals for the Second District, Marshall handed Charles Houston's dream over to the staff of the NAACP's legal defense department which, over the years, he had built up. In July, 1965, President Johnson appointed Judge Marshall, United States Solicitor General—the government's chief lawyer.

Anthony Lewis, a noted authority in the history of law, has summed up the work of Thurgood Marshall's quarter of a century in a meaningful phrase. He calls him "one of the great creators of race-relations law that gave concrete meaning to the Constitution's generalities."

5 / *Tired Feet and Rested Hearts*

Where is tomorrow born? How does the future start?
On a winter working day. In a Negro woman's heart.

In Montgomery, Alabama, the line is drawn.
In Montgomery, Alabama, darkness into dawn.

Jim Crow on the buses. Don't get aboard.
Walk, walk, walk with the Lord!

EVE MERRIAM / *Montgomery, Alabama, Money, Missis-*
sippi, and Other Places

Jim Crow! The separate and unequal treatment of Negro Americans began with the Black Codes of slavery. These Codes were the rules adopted in every slave state regarding "human property" in relation to the public. The Codes said little about the treatment of a bondsman by his master except that a slave was not to be beaten to death by his owner except in self-defense, was not to be denied food to the point of actual starvation.

The Black Codes were concerned with keeping the slave safe for the master and subject to his master's commands. A slave was, therefore, forbidden to travel on public roads without a pass. The codes made escape difficult by declaring it a crime to harbor a slave, a crime to teach a slave to read or write, a crime for more than five slaves to assemble together, and a crime for a minister of the Gospel to marry slaves, since the offspring of a slave mother became the property of the master. The Codes made it illegal for a slave to be called as a witness in court even in his own defense.

It was expected that the close of the war and Emancipation would see the Black Codes disappear. Not at all! In 1866, the eleven states which had been in rebellion agreed to abide by the Thirteenth Amendment to the Constitution which abolished slavery forever, but it never occurred to their legislators to do away with the separate rules of behavior for those who had been held in servitude. There were a very few differences in the new Black Codes. Freedmen could now enter into legal marriage, they could bear witness in court, though not sit on juries. They had limited freedom of movement, *if* they could show that they were employed by a white person. Their children were their own to raise and love. The chief difference, however, was that they were called "freedmen" instead of slaves. Freedmen but not free men!

Congress refused to accept the states with their Black Codes back into the Union, and made clear what Emancipation was intended to mean by adding the Fourteenth Amendment in 1866 to the Constitution. Until a state agreed to abide by the new Amendment, it remained under military control. The Fourteenth Amendment forbade a state to deprive any person within its jurisdiction the equal protection of the laws. The Fifteenth Amendment, added in 1870, guaranteed that no citizen be denied the right to vote "on account of race, color, or previous condition of servitude."

For about ten years, under the Reconstruction Act and the presence of Federal troops, the eleven newly-constituted state governments were elected by voters, Negro and non-Negro. It appeared that slavery, in all its forms, had been banished from the continent. (Canada had never had slaves and Mexico had abolished slavery in 1824.)

A Civil Rights Bill passed by Congress in 1875 made it impossible to discriminate against Negro citizens in eating places, hotels, theaters, on trains, or ships at sea. And the United States troops were on hand in every state to see that the law was enforced.

Then, in 1877, the occupying army was withdrawn. The former slaves had only the protection of the Constitution and the Amendments. Words on paper. In place of legal Black Codes in the South, a system of "custom and tradition" had grown up, enforced, at first, by the secret terror and violence of the white-sheeted night riders—the Ku Klux Klan—or red-shirted Vigilantes. Within a few years, customary segregation was replaced by legal segregation. With skill and determination, the whites found loopholes by which to deprive the Negroes of the privilege of voting: a "grandfather clause," exempting from voting tests anyone whose grandfather could vote in 1800; a poll tax beyond the Negro's power to pay; a private "white" primary; some tricks at registration time; and, if needed, a ballot box with a false bottom. In 1883, the Supreme Court had removed the protection of the Civil Rights Act of 1875. In 1896, the Court went further. It was not discrimination, the judges said, if separate accommodations on railroads were made equal. The "equal" part of the decision was promptly lost in a race for separation.

Jim Crow rose from his shallow grave, bigger and stronger than ever before. He carried a rope in one hand and a policeman's club in the other. Segregation law was heaped upon segregation law. Making signs, WHITE and COLORED, kept the printers busy. "White" schools were housed in fine brick buildings, "black" schools in shacks and discarded barns. "White" railroad cars were equipped with diners and Pullmans. Dirty coaches marked "Colored" were up front by the engine.

The cities built Jim Crow public libraries which Negroes couldn't enter—not even to borrow books they'd written themselves! Separate seats in the courtrooms (but none in the jury box, for no Negroes were called for jury duty). Separate sections in street cars and buses, separate *but not equal.* Every day, every hour, for fifty years, Negro Americans were reminded that they were nobodies in the only world they knew.

That is the way it was in most of the South, a hundred years ago. And that is the way it was in 1956, two years after the 1954 United States Supreme Court had declared that separate could never be considered equal. That's the way it was in Montgomery, Alabama.

Rosa Lee Parks

Montgomery, Alabama, a pretty city, small as American cities go today, had a long history which filled its citizens, those who were white, with pride. They enjoyed showing tourists the capitol building with the American flag flying above the dome. (In 1955, when Rosa Lee Parks was a name unknown except to her family and friends, the stars and stripes still flew above the capitol. But the Confederate flag is raised there today.) Yet, even before 1955, residents never failed to point out the building nearby, where secession from the United States was voted in 1861 —"The Cradle of the Confederacy," they called it. Visitors were driven along the broad, shaded streets, past the library (for whites only), and the green campus of the small Methodist College, and the handsome homes set in spacious lawns and colorful gardens.

If the visitors happened to have an interest in the condition of the black citizens (who made up almost half of the city's population), they might be shown the public housing project (for colored) built just before World War II when so many sharecroppers left the plantations and poured into the city that there was simply no more room in "colored town." Or they might be driven past the green campus of Alabama State College, for Negro students. Almost certainly, the enquiring tourist would be told "Our Negroes are happy. They know their place. No sign of the discontent you hear so much about. In Montgomery, our race relations have always been good."

What would Negro Americans in Montgomery have to complain about? Didn't they have their own schools, their own churches, their own teachers and lawyers and doctors, their own social clubs? They weren't troubled by "outside agitation," and they had more sense than to raise a fuss about voting or to get excited by Supreme Court decisions against segregation. Buses brought the cooks and gardeners across town every morning to work.

Montgomery was not an industrial city—there weren't many other jobs open to colored people, but a few worked downtown as elevator operators and janitors in the office buildings and banks. Even the department stores employed a few of the more intelligent—not as salespeople, of course, but as lunchroom waitresses and bus boys and as seamstresses doing alterations in the ladies dress department.

Rosa Parks was one of the "lucky" ones. For several years, she had had a job at Montgomery's best department store as a seamstress. The middle-aged woman was an expert with her needle, trim and neat, with a quiet and genteel manner. Her customers were as gracious and friendly with her as they were with their maids at home. Some even asked for "Rosa" to fit them. She was popular with the store clientele.

The job paid better than being a domestic worker, and Mrs. Parks had to help out the family income. She had a sick mother to care for and three children, and her husband was often out of work. When she got home at night, there was the housework to do, and sometimes extra sewing for customers who brought work to her house. And there were meetings to attend. Mrs. Parks was the secretary of the local NAACP.

The regular meetings and the Board meetings took up time, but Mrs. Parks enjoyed hearing Ed Nixon and Reverend Seay discuss the current news. They had so much more time to read than she had. And, there was that young minister from Atlanta who had come to the Dexter Avenue Baptist Church . . . So young and so brilliant, he brought a breath of the outside world to their gatherings. What was it Reverend King had said about time being neutral? About human progress never rolling on its own wheels? "Only through the persistent effort of the work of men willing to be co-workers with God." Wasn't that how he had put it?

Rosa Parks tried to recall the speech while she was on the bus going home one Thursday evening in December. She had waited longer than usual at the bus stop and had stepped up hurriedly in the front to pay her fare, then dismounted and rushed to get to the side door where the Negroes entered. The bus was almost full—the Negroes filled the back seats, the whites the front, as always. At first, Mrs. Parks thought she'd have to stand for the long ride home. But one seat was vacant in the front of the Negro section—"the blind man's row" it was called, because it was considered "colored" or "white," depending on which end of the bus was more crowded. She settled down thankfully, realizing that she was very tired. Thursday was always a hard day at the store.

It was dark already—too dark to see anything out of the window. December days were so short. She relaxed and her mind had drifted to last night's meeting at church and Martin Luther King's talk about co-workers with God. It was a phrase the principal at her boarding school had often used. She hadn't heard talk like that for a long time.

There were overtones in Reverend King's voice, too, that reminded her of the New England principal—understandably. The young minister had been educated in Boston.

"I'd like to see Boston myself someday," Rosa Parks daydreamed. She had never been out of the South, and the teachers at the missionary school in Montgomery had talked so much about their home. The years spent at the boarding school, when she first came to Montgomery, had been the happiest of her life. It was during the war, when it looked as if things were getting better for the people, what with all the promises of the Four Freedoms and the President's wife being so understanding and all. But it hadn't turned out that way—not in Montgomery at any rate. If anything, things had gotten worse.

"Move back—don't you see a white man standing in the aisle?" The voice of the bus driver broke into Rosa Parks' reverie. "You there, in the middle seats—I'm speaking to you."

The other Negroes stood and moved to the back.

A half-buried question forced itself to the front of Mrs. Parks' mind. "Why do we have to crowd in the back of the buses anyway, when we pay the same as other people?"

Somebody had figured out that seventy percent of the bus riders were Negroes on this route, and they had less than half the seats. It wasn't fair.

"Hurry up there."

Rosa Parks felt that the eyes of everybody in the bus were on her—dark, worried eyes from the back, the cold blue eyes of the man towering above her. His gray coatsleeve brushed her arm impatiently. He was young and husky—and she was tired, tired as could be.

"No!" Her voice, usually so softly modulated, rang out very loud.

She hadn't really made up her mind to disobey the order, but the word had slipped out. It was said now. She did not move.

The bus driver half rose from his seat, thought better of it, slammed the vehicle in gear, and drove to the next stop. He left the bus standing—and there was a deep, worried silence in the back seats. Then Rosa heard a sigh and "O Lord" in the cracked voice of an old man in back of her. A policeman stalked in and seized her by the shoulder. She was under arrest.

With such dignity as she could muster, trim and composed, as if she were dismounting for a shopping expedition or going to church, Mrs. Parks stepped off the bus ahead of the policeman. He clapped handcuffs on her wrist and, ten minutes later, she was on the way to jail.

It was after nine o'clock before she was allowed to put in a telephone call. The guard leaned against the wall and glared.

Mrs. Parks had submitted quietly to questioning, to having her fingerprints taken, to hearing herself charged with disturbing the peace. She had let herself be locked in a filthy prison cell without complaint.

One call! Rosa considered. It had better be to her husband, Ray. He would be so worried when she didn't come home from work on time. But what if he couldn't find a lawyer? The NAACP legal counsel no longer lived in Montgomery. There was only Virginia Durr's husband to turn to, and the Durrs were white. Poor Ray! He had no use for white people—with good reason, considering his boyhood experiences. Suppose he refused to tell Clifford

Durr she was in jail? Suppose Mr. Durr failed her? It would be safer to call Ed Nixon, her neighbor. For the length of time it took to dial the number, Rosa Parks panicked. Then, suddenly, as clearly as if he were standing beside her, she heard young Reverend King's voice saying "co-worker with God."

This arrest of hers could be the God-sent push to get the wheels of progress going for the Negro people of Montgomery. Every day, people less fortunate than herself had to listen to abuse by the bus drivers. She knew from the NAACP records how many arrests there were every month.

In the time it took for Ed Nixon to answer the phone, she had calmly made up her mind that something good might come of her trouble. She didn't know what, but she had a feeling that maybe she ought not to ask for bail at all—ought to stay right in the horrid, bug-ridden cell. The people were not going to get any change in their condition without protest and suffering. "If it has to be somebody, it might as well be me."

Several hours passed before the summons to the police sergeant's office came. Rosa Parks had made no effort to sleep. Sitting upright on the edge of her bunk, she had time to think more clearly, but she had not changed her mind. She didn't know how, but she was sure that staying in jail could be useful.

It was all very well for the NAACP leaders up North to fight for big issues like desegregating schools and the right to buy a house in any part of town you could pay for. Those things were so far in the future for her people in Montgomery that they watched from a distance, never raising their voices, never even complaining of their lot where white people could hear them. "You can't keep a job if you go around with a chip on your shoulder," one of the women on the NAACP Board had said last year when Reverend Seay wanted to do something about opening up the schools. But the segregation on the buses that everyone had to ride—the insults, the daily humiliation, the jailings—were something the poorest, the least educated could understand. If staying in jail would help change this one condition of their lives, Mrs. Parks was ready.

"Lawyer outside to see you," the guard grumbled, and jerked open the door of her cage.

Four people were waiting in the office. Her husband, both Mr. and Mrs. Durr, and a neighbor, Ed Nixon. Nixon was a Pullman porter who made the run from Chicago to New Orleans. He was an officer in Philip Randolph's union, but he had a house in Montgomery and was able to be home with his family a couple of days a month.

"Had a hard time persuading him," Ed Nixon said with a jerk of his head toward Mr. Parks. "He's bull-headed, but he came around, and I went with him to see Mr. Durr." (Clifford Durr sometimes handled cases for the Brotherhood of Sleeping Car Porters and Maids.)

The Durrs were an old Alabama family, but Clifford Durr had spent years in Washington. He had had an important job in President Roosevelt's administration. He had only been back in Montgomery the last year or so. Rosa Parks had not met Mr. Durr, but she considered his wife a real friend. She did sewing for Mrs. Durr and her half-grown girls—mostly making over things which relatives had given them—for the Durrs didn't have much more to live on than she and her husband did.

Mrs. Durr was Alabama-born, too—from Birmingham. But she didn't act like any white Southern lady Rosa Parks had ever laid eyes on. She was more like the northern teachers in the Mission boarding school, but even easier to talk to. When she brought things to the house to be altered, or when Mrs. Parks brought finished work back, after they'd finished their business, they would visit over a cup of tea.

That was how Virginia Durr heard about Reverend Seay getting Mrs. Parks a scholarship to Highlander Adult School last year. When Rosa Parks thought she couldn't make it because of the train fare, Virgina Durr had scurried around and collected the money for her ticket and bought her a bathing suit for a going-away present because she said Highlander had a big swimming pool.

The week-long workshop on citizenship at the interracial school had been a high point of Rosa Park's life. *Negro Americans and whites and Indians from India, all studying together in friendship as human beings should.* And now Mrs. Durr was seeing her in this humiliating condition, rumpled and grimy from the dirty cell of a Jim Crow jail.

She clung for a moment to her husband, but it was Virginia Durr's shoulder she cried on.

"I'm not crying for myself," she stammered as she rubbed the tears off her cheeks. "It wasn't just being told to give up my seat to a white man on the bus. It's everything that happens to our people day in and day out. Why can't we be treated like ordinary individuals? It's not me so much as the others—the ones the police hit over the head for no reason, the ones who won't have a lawyer to represent them in court. It's the whole unbearable Jim Crow living. Week after week. Year after year. If it will do any good, I'll just stay here in jail."

"It's already done good, that 'No' of yours has," Ed Nixon answered gravely. "You've started something! The word of your arrest is sweeping through the community. The ministers—AME Zion and Baptists together—they're calling a big mass meeting for tomorrow night. Maybe it's time our people stopped riding the buses."

"A—a boycott?" Rosa Parks raised up her head in pride. Nixon had often talked boycott as a means of protest. He knew its value from his experience in the union. "To protest my arrest?"

"As an 'Amen' to your 'No,'" Virginia Durr said. This was the first she had heard of the mass meeting. "But how will the people get to work Monday morning?" Mrs. Durr asked Ed Nixon worriedly.

"Walk."

"But it's three miles for some—way across town."

"And three miles back. It will be a twenty-four hours boycott."

Rosa Parks drew a deep breath. She no longer wanted to stay in jail. She wanted to be out there walking with the multitude. She wanted to be at that mass meeting to hear one of the ministers call for the boycott.

"You'll be there," Clifford Durr promised. "Bail is arranged for. I'm afraid, though, you'll have to wait until the banks open in the morning."

"You mean my wife can't get out of this place tonight?" It was the first time Ray Parks had said a word. All his distrust of white men, with their laws and customs, welled up in his voice. What was the use of lowering yourself to ask the help of a white lawyer if he couldn't get your wife out of jail?

Rosa Parks put her hand gently on his arm. "Don't worry, Ray. It's for the best I'm in this place. Don't you understand—it's not for just a seat on a bus—not any longer. The wheels are turning for change, and I've been permitted to be a co-worker with God!"

On Friday evening, the church was filled and three thousand people stood outside an hour before their meeting began. Most of the Negro ministers in town sat on the platform. And, in the neat blue suit she was accustomed to wearing to work, Rosa Parks sat with them. She was next to Reverend Seay, who was old, but young in spirit.

"I don't have to speak, do I?" she whispered.

"You've already said it," he smiled. "That 'No' of yours is ringing in their ears."

It was true. She didn't have to explain or apologize for being in jail. Her being on the platform was enough.

The audience sang "Onward Christian Soldiers, Marching As To War."

"But it's not war we want, but peace—with freedom," she thought.

Now the chairman said "It's time to act. Let's act."

Ed Nixon told briefly the meaning of a boycott, the way it was used by union men.

"Jim Crow buses." Rosa Parks' mind ran ahead of the speakers' words.

Reverend Abernathy rose, big booming voice, broad shoulders.

"*Could have been a prize fighter; wrestles with our souls instead,*" Rosa Parks said to herself.

Now Reverend Seay was having his say.

"*How long has he been at it, this old Freedom Fighter?*"

Martin Luther King, Jr. was the last. Mrs. Parks kept her eyes on the crowd as King began.

"There comes a time when people get tired. We are here this evening to say to those who have mistreated us for so long: we are tired of being segregated and humiliated. Tired of being kicked about by the brutal feet of oppression. Now we have no alternative but to protest. We have sometimes given our white brothers the feeling we liked the way we are being treated. But we come here tonight to be saved from the patience that makes us patient with anything but freedom and justice."

Rosa Parks drew a deep breath. "*That's what I meant when I refused to give up my seat. I understand myself better when you explain it. Keep talking, Martin Luther King. Show us the road to Freedom,*" she thought.

"We will not resort to violence. We will not degrade ourselves with hatred. Love will be returned for hate!"

There was much to do between that Friday night and Monday morning. To be sure of empty buses meant reaching all the twenty thousand workers who rode to work every day, and other people beside the workers, too—the men and women out of jobs who might take a bus downtown to look for work, the housewives who might have chosen Monday to do a little Christmas shopping. *Everybody* must be told. Twenty ministers agreed to announce the boycott from their pulpits on Sunday. King volunteered to write a leaflet. It would have to be mimeographed and distributed house to house, church to church. Mrs. Parks offered to organize women and high school boys and girls for this job. She was at it until late Sunday evening. Monday morning, at six, she walked out of her front door, in her suit and hat and fresh white gloves, to take her place in the stream of workers tramping down the sidewalk.

The early morning air held a December chill. The pace was fast at first—too fast for the stout, elderly women carrying aprons in paper bags. (Some had thought to bring bedroom slippers that they could slip on in the white folks' kitchens, to rest tired feet.) The line slowed down to the pace of the older women.

The buses rolled by, stopped at their usual corners. The drivers scowled at the sidewalk parade walking past and started up again, without passengers. The news of the mass meeting had been printed in the *Montgomery Advertiser*, the city's big newspaper. The bus drivers were furious. They had also been unbelieving.

"After all," the dispatcher said, "how can they get to work without the bus? They've got to eat, don't they? Don't worry, you'll have riders. Wait and see."

But they had no riders. Seventeen thousand Negroes stayed off the buses that first day.

Mrs. Parks walked as if she had wings on her heels. She had to be at the store when it opened. Work would be piled up in the sewing room from the two days she'd missed. But when she did get to work, the manager of the department was waiting for her, tight lipped.

"You needn't take your hat off. We've got a girl in your place. A *white* girl. I must say I'm disappointed in you, Rosa. Getting yourself in jail. You always seemed quiet and respectable. I suppose that NAACP put you up to it."

There was quite a bit more abusive talk before Rosa Parks was told to go to the cashier's cage to pick up her wages for the five days she'd worked last week.

"You don't deserve to be paid at all—leaving all that Friday and Saturday work undone."

So, she was out of a job—for getting her name in the paper.

"The only time we do get our names printed is when we get in trouble with the law," she said to herself, and then remembered that love was to be returned for hatred. Reverend King's philosophy would take some practice. It was hard to think lovingly of the people that had put her out of work. She wondered how much more they would pay the white woman who had taken her place. Ed Nixon said it was mainly a matter of economics—*they keep us down so they can have a cheap supply of labor*. Did they understand what they were doing to millions of human beings? Or had they drifted into their ways unthinking? Were the whites caught in the trap of history along with their victims?

"*As I would not be a slave, so I would not be a master.*" Abraham Lincoln had said that. It had been printed on cardboard on the wall of the boarding school, along with other famous quotations. Rosa Parks had not thought of it for years. But maybe this was part of what Martin Luther King was preaching. "To free us will free those who call themselves masters." She had time for a lot of thinking on the long, lonely walk back home.

Another mass meeting was held in church that night. It

had needed no advertising. People came together to discuss their experiences. The twenty-four-hour boycott had been amazingly successful. Ninety-eight percent of the usual riders had stayed off the Jim Crow buses. Nevertheless, the bus company managment had refused even to meet with the committee of Negro clergymen or to listen to their very modest requests. All the Negroes were asking was that black bus riders be given courteous treatment; that all bus riders be seated on a first come, first served basis, Negroes from the back, whites from the front as usual; and lastly, that Negro drivers be hired on the routes serving the sections of town where Negroes lived. Desegregation of the buses? It had not even been mentioned. But still the powers that be in Montgomery were outraged.

"We'll just have to keep on walking." The crowds in the churches spoke with one voice. "We'll stay off the Jim Crow buses till the company feels it in its pocketbook. We'll walk if it takes a week—or two weeks!"

A week? Fifty thousand Negro Americans were called on to walk for a solid year before the victory was won.

This thing, the leaders realized that first night of the boycott, was bigger than the NAACP or the responsibility of any one church congregation. Every Negro in Montgomery had a part to play. A new organization was formed, the *Montgomery Improvement Association*. Martin Luther King, new in town and only twenty-six years old, was elected president. Nightly meetings in the various churches kept up the spirits of the people. The meetings also gave King and the other leaders an opportunity to teach the meaning of non-violent mass protest to people who had never heard of Mahatma Ghandi's Salt March to the Indian Ocean which had been the beginning of freedom from Colonial rule in far-off India. Nor had they heard of the New Englander, Henry David Thoreau, who had gone to prison as a protest against the government's support of slavery before the Civil War. Through Martin Luther King, Jr., Ghandi and Thoreau became familiar names.

Peaceful mass action as a means of freeing Negro Americans from the humiliation of segregation was not a new idea when King began to preach it in Montgomery. It had been advanced as a means of protest by Philip Randolph and, later, by the president of Howard College. A few young Negroes in the NAACP had even tried it in a small way in Oklahoma. But it was King, that long year in Montgomery, who developed peaceful mass action as a technique, and more than a technique—a deeply felt belief on the part of the laborers, the cooks and maids and truck drivers, the doctors and teachers, that in this way, and this way alone, could they tear down the wall that Jim Crow had built between themselves and their white-skinned neighbors.

"The most important thing," King wrote, when the battle had been won, "is what has happened to the Negro. For the first time, the Negro is on his own side. This had not always been true. But today the Negro is with himself. He has gained a new respect for himself. World opinion is on his side. The law is on his side. The Negro is eternally through with segregation. He will never accept it again, in Alabama, Mississippi, Georgia, or anywhere else."

This is what Rosa Parks' "No" had meant. It is what the walkers were saying all that first winter as they trudged to work and home again on tired feet. To walk, to keep eyes forward and hearts free of hate when insults—and rotten eggs—were thrown in their path, to go proudly to jail for the cause of freedom, to suffer violence and give understanding and compassion in return, could only have been learned under inspired leadership. This inspiration Martin Luther King gave not only by eloquent speeches, but also by suffering with the others the insults, the jailings, the physical violence, even the bombing of his own home.

"The non-violent man is he who not only refuses to fight, but refuses to accept wrong, and refuses to hate those who wrong him."

Christmas went by—a strange Christmas in Rosa Parks' home, for there was no money for presents, no time for festivity. As on other days, she went to headquarters to man the telephone or the car pool. (For cooks and butlers in wealthy households, Christmas is merely another work day.)

The New Year, 1956, came in with rain and mud. Through the winter weather the dark-skinned citizens of Montgomery tramped. Empty buses waited in vain for passengers. The bus company attacked the boycott with every weapon at hand. White gangs in cars rode alongside the marchers, harassing, shouting, cursing. The few sympathetic whites such as the Durrs or Reverend Goetz, who wanted to help, had to act with caution lest they make matters worse. Non-whites who had cars—be they the Cadillacs of the doctors or undertakers, or rattletrap trucks or jalopies—cruised the streets picking up those who, for some reason, needed quick transportation. The volunteer drivers were arrested on trumped-up traffic charges. Domestic workers soon learned to pretend that they had nothing to do with such things as boycotts, pretend that is, if they wanted to keep their jobs.

Still, the people walked and, every night, they met together to plan, to pray, to sing "Onward, Christian Soldiers," "Nobody Knows the Trouble I've Seen," and "Walk Together Children."

"How can they keep it up?" a whole world wondered and an old woman answered. "My feets is tired," she said, "but my soul is rested."

When the bus company refused even to discuss the situation with the Association, the people voted to drop their very mild requests, to ask for nothing less than an end to segregated seating on the city buses.

Over the country, eighteen million Negro Americans kept their eyes on Montgomery. Mrs. Parks had said the word for all of them. What was happening in one small southern city could change their lives. In New York, in Chicago, in Memphis, in New Orleans, in Tallahassee, and in the cities of the far west, the voice of the soft-spoken seamstress became familiar through radio and TV. And Martin Luther King was on the way to becoming the most popular civil rights leader in America.

The attention and sympathy the walkers were receiving in the outside world became insufferable to the powers-that-be of Montgomery. They raked up an old, seldom-used law against boycotts, and summoned a grand jury. One February day, the Montgomery police arrested one hundred of the Negro leaders, including King and Rosa Parks. The charge was conspiracy.

For the second time in her life, Mrs. Parks found herself in the police station. "First they arrest us for riding their buses, then they arrest us for not riding," Ed Nixon said as he waited in line next to Rosa Parks to be finger-printed.

"At least it feels better when you're not alone," she answered.

Martin Luther King was tried first and was given a sentence of 386 days at hard labor. He appealed the decision of the court, and the trials of the ninety-nine others were put off until the higher courts could rule.

But, even with the leaders in jail, the mass walks did not stop for a day.

Spring came, and soft Alabama breezes were heavy with the fragrance of jonquils and tea olive blossoms. Robert Carter, NAACP lawyer and assistant to Thurgood Marshall, came South for a conference. He suggested bringing the problem of segregation on city buses to the Federal District Court on the grounds that people paying equal fare but not given equal treatment were being denied their rights under the Constitution. With long jail sentences hanging over them in the State Court, the leaders agreed to this course of action.

May passed and June came in—hot and sultry. The mass of Montgomery's Negro citizens continued walking. On the fourth of June, the verdict was handed down in the Federal Court: separate seating in city buses could not, under the Constitution of the United States, be upheld.

It was too soon, however, for a victory celebration. The city of Montgomery and the lawyers for the bus company appealed immediately to the Supreme Court. It was too soon to stop walking.

Months later, on December 21st, the Supreme Court upheld the District Court's decision, and bus segregation was outlawed not only in Montgomery, but everywhere in the United States.

The Christmas season was over and the beginning of another year at hand. Rosa Parks, her blue suit trim and neat as always, but showing its age, stepped into the bus and took a seat in the very front. She was on her way downtown to look for a job.

It took more courage than she had expected it would to meet the cold eyes and deadpan faces of the white women across the aisle. The law was on her side but, as Virginia Durr had said, when she came with her husband to pay a call on Christmas, a law is no good unless it's put to use. The Negroes were riding the buses again, but only a brave few were willing to risk unpleasantness in the front seats.

The first few days, before Reverend King went away, had been different. Then groups were assigned to ride the buses together, to test the law. But Martin Luther King had resigned the pastorate of the Dexter Avenue Church and moved back to Atlanta. And Reverend Abernathy was leaving, too. They were needed, of course, to open offices of the Southern Christian Leadership Conference. The Montgomery idea was taking root other places, the movement was spreading like a fast-growing tree. But here, in Montgomery, there had been a letdown. As if getting a seat in the front of a bus was glory enough!

In the meetings during the boycott, the speakers on the platform had conjured up visions of America as a Promised Land. If the people would only hold out and keep walking, parks, playgrounds, libraries, theatres, and schools would open to everybody.

A smile came to Mrs. Parks eyes, but didn't get as far as her mouth before it faded. "Even if the restaurants were desegregated," she said grimly to herself, "we couldn't eat at most of them. Not a dozen colored people in town make decent wages."

She realized, suddenly, that what had been accomplished that year was only a beginning. What she couldn't guess —what no one, in spite of the TV and the newspaper headlines, could have imagined, was that a nation-wide revolt would be dated from the moment when Rosa Parks said "No" to a bus driver's demand that she get up and give a white man her seat.

Rosa Parks did not get a job that day, nor on any of the days and weeks and months that she lived in Montgomery. Too many people who had jobs to give knew her name; too many recognized the face that had appeared on national television. The act that made her an honored figure in the rest of the country prevented her earning a living in the city she knew and loved. Mrs. Parks stayed in Montgomery for two more years, then she realized that she and her family would have to move away.

Today in Montgomery, over the state capitol, the Confederate flag flies, a tragic symbol of hate and the determination of a powerful few to kill a dream. The Negro Americans of Montgomery—until the Selma-to-Montgomery march of March, 1965 took place—were discouraged, rather lonely. Yet, in their hearts, they knew that their 300,000-mile march had transformed the Cradle of the Confederacy into the cradle of a new hope for brotherhood.

And Rosa Parks? In a big Northern city, she quietly goes to work every day as a seamstress and watches, with tremendous pride, as Americans—black and white together—continue the struggle for fulfillment of the old dream.

"The only way to get a thing done is to start to do it," she says when people ask, as they still do ask, why she spoke up that December day. "You start, then keep on doing it, and finally, you'll find it's finished, even if in the beginning you think you can't do it at all."

Back in 1956, when Mrs. Parks said "No!" to a startled bus driver, she started something far bigger than she or anybody else could have imagined. When she returned briefly to Montgomery as a speaker at the triumphant Freedom Rally in March of 1965, Reverend Ralph Abernathy spoke no more than the truth when he introduced her to the twenty thousand freedom fighters as "the First Lady of the Movement."

6 / At the Point of a Bayonet

As if it harmed me
Giving others the same chances and rights as myself—
As if it were not indispensable
To my own rights that others have the same.

WALT WHITMAN / *Thoughts*

Long before the days of the Civil War, Negro women walked the Freedom Road. Nameless grandmothers, remembering Africa and a time before slavery; young mothers fleeing to the woods with their infants, choosing to live—or die—hunted in the forest, if only they could save their children from being sold as chattel like horses or pigs or rugs on the floor. Girls, scarcely out of their teens walking with their men, or ahead of their men, to freedom.

Harriet Tubman and Sojourner Truth, two women who had been born slaves, devoted all their strength to freeing others. Illiterate, penniless, homely, in turban and cast-off clothes, that was Harriet Tubman. Her name has become a synonym for majestic courage. In the generation after Emancipation, Mary Church Terrell, Ida Wells Barnett, and Mary McLeod Bethune were heroic Freedom Fighters. Cast from the same mold were the educators, Mrs. Daisy Lampkin of North Carolina and Mrs. Septima Clark of South Carolina, who gave up her teaching career rather than deny her membership in the NAACP. And there were the nameless heroines who worked all day as domestic servants and then trudged home at night to wash and iron clothes for their own children to wear the next day to school. The central idea, the driving force in the lives of hundreds of Negro women was that their own sons and daughters might have the education denied to themselves.

In our time there are the stalwarts like Ella Baker, adult advisor of the Student Non-violent Coordinating Committee; like Diane Nash Bevel and Gloria Richardson who served prison terms in defense of civil rights; and Rosa Parks who was prepared to stay in a Montgomery jail if it would help to break the barriers of discrimination for others. Sparking the Mississippi Freedom Democratic Party today are Mrs. Fannie Lou Hamer, Mrs. Victoria Gray, Mrs. Annie Devine, Mrs. Johnnie Lee Walker.

With this tradition in American history, it is not surprising to find a Negro woman, Mrs. Daisy Bates of Little Rock, Arkansas, in the forefront of the struggle to open the schools.

Daisy Bates

"Read that last part aloud, L.C. I can't believe my eyes. Maybe I can believe my ears." Daisy Bates, from her favorite position on the hearth rug, at her husband's feet, held out the evening paper, dated May 17, 1954. Sitting there, small, slender, pretty enough to be called beautiful, Mrs. Bates looked more like a college girl than a successful newspaper woman and state president of the NAACP.

Her husband obligingly took the newspaper. It headlined the news of the Supreme Court order ending segregation in the schools. He glanced down the right-hand column and began to read. "We conclude that in the field of education the doctrine of 'separate but equal' has no place. Separate is inherently unequal. . . ."

Mrs. Bates interrupted solemnly, "It's the second most wonderful thing that's happened to me in my whole twenty-nine years."

"What's the first?" L. C. Bates was amused as always by his wife's youthful enthusiasm.

"Making you fall in love with me," she answered promptly. "But think what the decision means for the whole country, for the children growing up without having to feel themselves nobodies. And for the white children, too."

"Integration is still just on paper, Daisy. The white folks down here are going to hate it."

Bates had been born in Mississippi, but he had grown up and been educated in Ohio and had begun his work as a newspaper man there. He was a great deal older than his wife, as anxious for change as she was. However, long experience had trained him not to hope for too much.

"Hate integration? Not in Little Rock! Look at the next column lead. 'Governor Cherry says Arkansas will obey the law.' I think you ought to use Cherry's statement as the subject for your editorial this week. Or maybe I could go to the capitol building and ask the governor to give us an interview to print. It's going to make everything easy, having the government on our side. Don't you think so?"

The Bates spent the rest of the evening discussing just how to make the most of the great decision in their next issue of the paper. They had started the *State Press* years ago, only a year after they moved to Little Rock. From the first, it had been a crusading newspaper.

Daisy Bates had no children of her own, but she had made the children of the Negro community in Little Rock her special concern. Under her husband's training, she had learned to watch for news items in the Northern press, especially the court cases in Washington being won by the NAACP legal department. The way she explained them in the columns of the *State Press* made her readers feel that democracy was coming to Arkansas.

Subscriptions to the paper rose from 10,000 to 20,000 to 50,000. Mrs. Bates, with her easy friendliness, reached out into the white community and persuaded the business men to advertise in the paper. Several professors from the University and the editor of the largest newspaper in Little Rock, Mr. Harry Ashmore, joined the NAACP and, presently, when an interracial Human Relations Committee came into being, Mrs. Bates, as editor of the *State Press*, was asked to join.

She felt she had good grounds for believing that Little Rock would set an example for the whole South in ending school segregation. Still, when the light in her bedroom was turned out after the evening's long discussion, she stared up at the ceiling, unable to sleep. She had faith that things would go well; yet far down in her memory lay troubling doubts.

"Who am I? What do I stand for?"

She remembered the very spot in Huttig, the small town where she was born, the spot where she first knew what it meant to have a dark skin. She was seven years old and had come to Huttig's only butcher shop, where everybody—black or white—did their trading, to buy chops for her mother. The butcher made her stand aside and wait for her order and plainly told her why. "You have to wait 'til I wait on the white people. Now take your meat and get out of here!"

That was a little thing, but there were more serious hurts, once she had been made aware. It all added up in time, and Daisy came to hate anybody with a white skin.

Then, when she was in her teens, her beloved foster-father took sick and lay dying of cancer in the Negro ward in the basement of Huttig's segregated hospital. He called her to his bedside and said, "You're filled with hatred. Hate can destroy you, Daisy. Don't hate white people just because they're white. If you hate, make it count for something. Hate the humiliations we are living under in the South. . . . Hate the insults hurled at us by white scum—and then try to do something about it or your hate won't spell a thing. . . . Daisy, nothing's going to change all of a sudden." (Lying there in the darkness, she could re-member every word the good old man had said.) "Any Negro speaking out alone will suffer. But more and more will join him, and the blacks, acting together will one day. . . ." Her father's voice trailed off. He had talked more later, but this part was what she liked to remember. It was the last time she had seen him. The next day, he had died.

That was in 1939. Two years later, she had married the man who had been her father's friend, and they had moved to Little Rock. At seventeen, Daisy Bates had very few possessions to bring along, but her father's parting words were a rich heritage. *Make your hate spell something.*

"What Daddy didn't foresee," Daisy thought serenely, "is that we no longer have to try to change things all alone. Nine white men in a courtroom and thousands more over America have begun to understand that Negro Americans have to be included in the promise of the Declaration of Independence and the Constitution. Good white people here in Little Rock see that. *Together* we'll work things out—like Daddy said."

This thought took firm hold of her and sustained her through the months and years to come.

Governor Cherry had said, "Arkansas will obey the law." In 1954, just five days after the Supreme Court's decision, one small Arkansas town, Fayetteville, announced that six Negro children would be admitted to the formerly all-white high school. A week later, another town opened its school to Negro children. Catholic private schools in two other towns integrated their classes. Proudly, Daisy Bates wrote about these events in the *State Press*. But what, she asked, about Little Rock? What about the capital city? The Committee on Human Relations asked, too. And so did Harry Ashmore, editor of the Arkansas *Gazette* and the Bates' good friend.

Mr. Virgil Blossom, Superintendent of the Little Rock School District, reported that he was ready with a timetable for the school board to follow. He was merely waiting for the Supreme Court to give specific directions. In late May, 1955, the school board received Virgil Blossom's plan and submitted it to the Federal District Court for its approval. Integration was to be carried through in three stages, beginning with the high schools, then junior high, finally the elementary schools. The first stage, Blossom stated, would begin as soon as the two new high school buildings, started last winter, were completed. He hoped no later than September, 1957. Full integration of the schools would be accomplished throughout the city within six years.

The Blossom plan, accepted by the District Court, was slower and less thorough than Mrs. Bates had hoped for, but she reminded those who were critical of it that no other city in the South had submitted any plan at all. "We, at least, have a definite date to look forward to: September, 1957. To see our young people march into high schools to get an education equal to the best—isn't that worth waiting for a little longer?"

There was some grumbling among prejudiced whites and Mrs. Bates noticed that the interracial groups seemed to meet less and less often, but she did not agree with the older people in the NAACP that trouble lay ahead. It was true, as her husband mentioned, that the new governor had not spoken out. But Daisy Bates did not lose faith.

"Look at Montgomery!" she said. The idea of fifty thousand people walking to work rather than riding the Jim Crow buses thrilled her. The Montgomery boycott would silence, once and for all, those who insisted that Negroes *liked* segregation. And the eloquent words of Martin Luther King, Jr. seemed to her like an echo of her own father. *Hate discrimination, not people.* Wasn't that the same as Dr. King's non-violent mass action carried on with love? It was too bad, of course, that the people in Montgomery had such a long, hard struggle just to ride with dignity on the buses. Here in Little Rock, she pointed out, the buses let Negroes sit where they pleased. Little Rock was different from the rest of the South!

"Don't worry, L.C." she said. "Everything will come out all right."

During his campaign for the governorship, Orval Faubus made desegregation of the schools an issue—the "Number One issue," he called it. But he "merely" questioned whether the state was ready for full and complete integration in the schools. True, his stand was not as good as Governor Cherry's had been as far as Daisy and L. C. Bates were concerned. Still, it expressed none of the hate of the White Citizens' Council.

"The election of Faubus should not make a difference," Daisy said to her husband. "Arkansas will integrate. Those who stand for defiance of the law do not have the excuse they use further South—that the problem is too big, that there are so many Negro students to enter the system. In Arkansas, our people make up only one-fourth of the population . . . a smaller proportion than in some Northern cities with good, mixed schools."

Mr. and Mrs. Bates watched the election campaign with as much interest as if they'd been running. It was true, as L. C. Bates mentioned, that Faubus was surrounding himself with segregationists. On the other hand, another candidate accused him of sitting on the fence, of not being strong enough about keeping Negroes out. Daisy Bates remained confident.

Daisy Bates' first real discouragement came in the late spring of 1956. In response to rising opposition to his plan, Virgil Blossom proposed modifications. Instead of opening *all* the high schools in the city, only Central High would be open to Negroes, and only to a very few of the number who had applied. And he no longer made mention of the six-year timetable. In fact, his amended plan didn't talk about junior high and elementary schools at all. Even the September, 1957 date stood in doubt.

Reluctantly, Mrs. Bates had to admit that the picture over the state looked less hopeful from day to day. When the local branch of the NAACP voted, in the name of three parents, to bring suit for immediate opening of the schools of Little Rock to Negro children, she gladly offered her assistance. The Legal Defense and Education Fund lawyers agreed to advise and carry their case to the highest court, if that became necessary. But Thurgood Marshall, who came down from New York for a consultation, explained that the first action would have to come from the parents concerned, and a local lawyer would have to be supplied.

Mrs. Bates went around making speeches and raising money for a lawyer. Mr. Wiley Branton, a very able attorney, offered to begin the action. His offer was accepted and the suit was brought in the Federal court in April.

The case was lost in the lower court and Mr. Branton and the NAACP immediately appealed to the Circuit Court of Appeals.

While they waited for a verdict, one good thing happened. In August, the State Board of Education announced the opening of all colleges under its jurisdiction to Negroes at the undergraduate level. On the other hand, White Citizens' Councils, such as Senator Eastland had started in Mississippi, were being openly organized in Arkansas. Their slogans were printed and scattered about the city. One evening, Daisy Bates found one on her doorstep: *"We are about to start a great crusade to return the control of government to the Anglo-Saxon people of the South."*

As if it had ever been taken away! As if affirming the rights that belonged to Negro citizens meant taking away the rights of others! Daisy Bates was heartsick.

There was more—much more—of the same sort of thing that summer. Violent arguments took place between segregationists and opponents of four measures designed to keep the Arkansas schools just as they were. The vote in November showed Mr. and Mrs. Bates what a hard road stretched ahead. Daisy Bates was not so much worried that Faubus was re-elected. The large vote in favor of the segregationist measures seemed to her more ominous. Orval Faubus still remained an unknown quantity—until the following spring.

On April 29, 1957, the Appeals Court announced its ruling on the suit brought by the parents of the Negro students. From one viewpoint, they lost, since the decision of the lower court was upheld. But this meant that the original Blossom plan was approved. High school integration must begin, as proposed, in September 1957. The time, which in 1955 had seemed too long away, was at hand. And the proposal to start with only one high school, which a year ago had seemed very limited, now seemed a good beginning.

But other trouble was brewing. Reaction! The NAACP was blamed for bringing up the case. Mrs. Bates became known as a "troublesome female" who stirred up Little Rock. Car loads of Klansmen from Georgia and Mississippi came into the city waving the Confederate flag. They circled the Bates' house, blowing horns and shouting. One night, when the Bateses had both been working late on the paper, they came from the *Press* office to find a cross burning in front of their picture window. Silently, L. C. Bates got out the garden hose, doused the flames, jerked out the smoldering sticks of wood, and tossed the thing into the gutter.

"I'm bringing trouble on you," his pretty wife said.

"Not you, Daisy, not you." He had seen violent men in action in Mississippi before Daisy had been born.

From the sixty students who had originally asked to transfer to Central High, Mr. Blossom had narrowed the list to thirteen. As trouble began, four more of the children dropped out. There were many reasons: fear, the threat that if the children persisted the parents might lose their jobs. Mrs. Bates blamed none of them. She was, however, very proud of the nine who stood staunchly for their right to get the best available schooling.

She spent most of her days that summer with the chosen nine and their parents. The older people were tense and anxious, and some of them were prepared to give up. The children were not.

"They'll like me when they get to know me," Terence Roberts said confidently. He was the oldest of seven children, an all-A student.

Ernest Green, who would enter the senior class, said he just *had* to go to Central High to get chemistry for college entrance. "There's no other way I can get to be a chemical engineer!"

Jefferson Thomas was a baseball player. He had been told by the school superintendent not to try out for the Central High team. Jeff had grinned and said he was willing to make the sacrifice. "Like Reverend King said, we have to suffer for liberty."

The six girls had spent weeks making new dresses to wear for the first day of school. Elizabeth Eckford, Thelma Mothershead, Carlotta Walls, Melba Pattilo, Glorio Ray, Minnijean Brown. Daisy Bates had come to know them very well. They were all so different and yet so alike in their determination. Later, after everything was over, people would speak of the nine Little Rock students as "tender warriors." Daisy Bates never thought of them this way. They understood and accepted their historic role as well as she did—as well as any adult. They knew that the thing they had undertaken was not for themselves alone. They wanted to enter Central High for a better education to be sure, but they would enter dreaming of "a world where all would know sweet freedom's way."

In August, segregationists suddenly took legal action. A bigoted group of women, calling themselves the Mother's League, went before Chancery Court and petitioned for a

temporary injunction forbidding all integration of the Little Rock schools. A surprise witness in support of their
petition was the governor of the state—Orval Faubus.

The injunction was granted.

"At last, we know which side Faubus is on," Mr. Bates
commented drily.

For twenty-four hours, the Klan and Citizen's Council
celebrated. Then Thurgood Marshall flew down from New
York; he and Wiley Branton went to court again. They
asked the Circuit Court, which had kept jurisdiction of the
Little Rock matter, to forbid interference with the court
order to open the school to the nine Negro students. On
August 30th, Federal Judge Ronald N. Davies ordered the
Little Rock School Board to proceed on schedule with its
plan and "enjoined all persons in any manner, directly or
indirectly, from interfering. . . ."

This order came just three days before the date set for
the opening of school. Would it be obeyed? What *was*
going to happen?

Mr. Ray, the father of one of the girls, came over that
night to ask Mrs. Bates some questions. He was wavering
in his decision to let his daughter be a part of this experiment in democracy.

"They'll be safe, won't they?" Gloria Ray's father asked,
pacing the floor of the Bates' living room.

Daisy Bates glanced at the picture window, taped up
where a rock, thrown by hoodlums, had cracked the glass.
"I don't know, Mr. Ray . . . I just don't know."

An editorial by Harry Ashmore in the *Gazette* the next
morning brought her some measure of assurance: "We do
not believe any organized group of citizens would undertake to do violence to school children of any race. If there

are any individuals who might embark on such a reckless and indefensible course, we have no doubt that our law enforcement officers can and will preserve order." Daisy clipped the editorial and showed it to each of the parents.

The next day—the day before school was to open—Governor Faubus acted. He made a speech on the Capitol steps saying that if the Negroes insisted on going ahead with integration, blood would run in the streets of Little Rock. Then he ordered the National Guard to surround Central High School "for the protection of life and property."

On September 3, the Little Rock schools opened. Negro students stayed away from Central High while the school board and the NAACP lawyers consulted with Judge Davies. Had the governor ordered out the soldiers to protect the Negro children? Was it *their* lives the governor meant to protect? Why then, Thurgood Marshall asked, had he declared the school grounds out of bounds for Negroes? And for the city police?

Judge Davies said that he had to assume good faith on the part of the governor. He ordered the children to enter Central High as planned.

On September 4, the afternoon this last court order came through, Virgil Blossom called the parents of the nine students to his office. (They wouldn't go without Daisy Bates, so she was present, uninvited.) The school superintendent was deeply disturbed. He could give little assurance that the children would be protected, but the court order must be obeyed. He instructed the parents *not* to accompany the children to school next morning. "If violence breaks out, it will be easier to protect the students if the adults aren't there."

Outside the superintendent's office, the little group

looked at one another. Could they send their children off tomorrow alone? Anxious eyes turned to Daisy Bates. If she said so, they would refuse, back down, give up the struggle. If she said "go ahead," the children would not hesitate. But would she, could she, ask the nine young people to fight the "Battle of Little Rock" alone?

It was almost dawn when Daisy Bates stumbled, exhausted, into bed. She had a plan but she still did not know if it would work. Reverend Crenshaw, a Negro minister and president of the local branch of the NAACP, had offered his church as a meeting place. In this way, the children could at least walk up to the school gates together. Talking with Crenshaw had given her an idea. What if ministers, white and black, walked with the children? Surely that would be some protection from a mob that claimed to be Christian.

She had called the Reverend Dunbar Ogden, Jr., a stranger to her, but president of the Ministerial Association. He hadn't lived in Little Rock long, but she had heard vaguely that he was sympathetic. Reverend Ogden would, he said, call some other ministers. He could make no promises. Next, she had called the city police and talked to the officer in charge. He agreed to send a police car to stand at the corner of Twelfth Street and Park Avenue. That was all he could do. City police were not allowed to come closer than Twelfth Street while the National Guard was "in occupation." It was past midnight when Daisy Bates began notifying the parents of the plan. She managed to reach all but one family. The Eckfords had no phone and lived far across town. She'd try again in the morning.

Daybreak came with a flood of calls from out-of-town

reporters, and with hostile cars parading past her door. At eight-fifteen, her husband brought the car around and Daisy Bates climbed in.

As they stopped at Twelfth Street, word came on the car radio that a mob had gathered around a Negro girl at Central High. Elizabeth Eckford! In the excitement, Mrs. Bates had forgotten to go by the Eckford's home to tell them of the change of plans. Bates leaped from the car and ran up the hill to see what he could do.

At the church, everything was going according to plan. The police were on hand. Reverend Ogden had come, and there was another white minister, a stranger who was on a visit from Nashville, and two Negro ministers. Daisy watched the little line form and start walking. Ogden and the AME Zion minister, Mr. Driver, in front, then the eight young people with the Nashville stranger and the other Negro minister as rear guard. A little apart, but ready if there was trouble, two men walked together. The younger one was David Ogden, the minister's son; the older, Lee Lorch, a white professor from Philander Smith College for Negroes. Daisy Bates had met Professor Lorch and his wife when she had taken a few courses at the college. Now he had come to be of service without being asked.

Numb with anxiety, she waited. Wild rumors were still coming over the radio that a fifteen-year-old Negro girl— it must be Elizabeth—had been turned away from Central High at the point of bayonets by the National Guard and had been attacked by a mob.

Mr. Bates returned, put his arm around his wife's shoulder.

"Elizabeth is safe, Daisy. I saw her getting on a Sixteenth Avenue bus. A white woman was with her. Mrs.

Lorch, I think. I couldn't get near enough to see. The hoodlums were milling around and yelling insults at a man they said had waited with the girl at the bus stop. He was a kindly-looking, gray-haired man. I heard a stringy-haired woman shout, 'Go back to New York, you Jew.' The crowd looked as if they might beat him, but they caught sight of a car with an Illinois license and a young Negro driver and ran off for other excitement. They hardly noticed the eight children and the ministers."

Very soon, the little procession returned to the church.

"They turned us away, Mrs. Bates," Ogden said. His head was held high, his eyes blazing with anger. "I asked why. The captain said, 'Governor Faubus' orders.' "

Daisy Bates nodded silently. She was trying to decide on the next move. The "Battle of Little Rock" was just beginning.

The outcome would hang in the balance for more than two years.

Until September 20, Governor Faubus used the state troops to defy the laws of the federal government. During those weeks, while the NAACP lawyers sought relief once again from the court, and the United States Attorney General and even the President tried peaceable persuasion, mobs rode unhindered through the Negro areas of Little Rock. In the presence of Faubus' army, the city police, the mayor, and the "good" people of Little Rock, the ones Daisy Bates counted on, were helpless to keep order.

The nine Negro children stayed away from school. Mrs. Bates visited them in their homes or had their parents bring them to her house where professors from Philander Smith College came to help them with their lessons. At night, parents of the children guarded their homes with shotguns ready. The Bates' house was guarded, too, by Mr. Bates and friends.

On Friday, September 20, the latest order came from Judge Davies. "The Governor does not have the power to use the National Guard to prevent a law from being carried out nor to create obstructions to the exercise by the Negro children of their rights as judicially declared."

That night, Governor Faubus sullenly withdrew his guardsmen. The mayor and city police had said they didn't need his troops. Let them keep order if they could! An anxious Saturday was spent by the city officials attempting to get the federal government to provide for the protection of the children by federal marshals. Nothing was accomplished. Sunday was declared a day of prayer for the city. The Mother's League called for an all-out demonstration when the Negro children came to school on Monday morning. Sunday night, having failed to get the promise of marshals, Virgil Blossom told Mrs. Bates, now the acknowledged leader of the Little Rock nine, to have the students at her house next morning, and to wait there for further instructions.

Once again, Mrs. Bates consulted with the parents in the middle of the night. Two Negro school principals went with her, for it was no longer safe to drive through Little Rock streets at night, alone.

"We'll meet at my house," she told the parents. "At the school, the city police have promised protection."

On Monday morning, all nine young people accompanied by their parents were at the Bates' home. Then, all of them except Mrs. Brown and Mr. Eckford had to leave for work. Photographers and reporters, Negro and white, were milling about and the radio was blaring threatening reports. The reporters had come from all over the country and several had stayed at the Bates home all night. The students sat listening silently, waiting for word from the police.

At last, the call came. The police would escort the cars after they were close to the school, but they would not come to escort them all the way from the Bates home. Tense with anxiety, the children and Mrs. Bates got into two waiting cars together with two young men who had volunteered to go along. As directed, they went by a round-about route to the side door of the school. Police hurriedly escorted the nine students inside, while the howling mass of men and women were diverted by a car of Negro reporters.

The students were inside Central High! Little Rock schools were integrated. The news was flashed to a waiting world.

Of the two thousand white children in the school, about fifty came rushing out. They were enough to set off the riot which police tried in vain to quiet.

Three hours after they had entered, the nine students were brought back by police to Daisy Bates' door.

The police reported that teachers and students inside the school had given no trouble. It was the outside mob the police feared. All night, the city was in their grip. Houses of Negro citizens were darkened, but volunteers guarded the homes of the children with guns. L. C. Bates and half a dozen friends patrolled the Bates home. Nevertheless, rocks and a bullet crashed through the window.

The children were kept out of school all the next day. In midafternoon, a battalion of airborne federal troops parachuted into Little Rock. The President of the United States had moved, at last, to enforce the Constitution!

Next morning, when Daisy Bates drove the first car full of children to Central High, she saw soldiers once more guarding the entrance with guns and bayonets. However, there was this difference: they were federal soldiers on hand to protect the Negro children and to enforce the Constitution and the law. The words her father had spoken so long ago echoed in Daisy Bates' mind with new meaning. *Nothing's going to change all of a sudden. . . . But more and more will join and the blacks, acting together, will one day. . . .* This day had come. But her father could not have imagined that it would take the United States Army acting *with* the Negroes to put nine children in school.

She started her car and drove thoughtfully home through the crowded, hate-filled streets. That night, another cross was burned in their yard. It didn't matter; the children were safe. They had returned to her home under military guard before the end of the day, pouring out reports of friendliness on the part of most of the white students. One girl had invited Minnijean to join the glee club. Several had invited them to eat lunch at their table.

"We're really in Central High!" Jefferson Thomas marveled.

The oldest of the group, Ernest Green, had said nothing.

"Aren't you happy that President Eisenhower sent the troops, Ernest?" Mrs. Bates asked.

"No. I'm glad to be getting a decent education, but I'm sorry integration had to come that way," he answered.

The United States soldiers were needed in Little Rock to

keep peace for the whole of the school year. The rioting mob was gradually quieted, but the hate of the segregationists was not stilled. The children felt it more and more in their classes as the weeks went by. The parents felt it. Many of them lost their jobs. But the hostility was visited most of all upon Daisy Bates and her husband. Their house was bombed three separate times. Merchants withdrew advertisements from their paper and subscribers were pressed to cancel their subscriptions.

But hardest for Daisy Bates to bear was the strain on the children. She, more than anyone else, had known the humiliations—and even physical attacks—they suffered. But the term was over at last.

Ernest Green, serious and unsmiling, the senior of the group, was graduated with his class and admitted to a good Midwestern university.

The last soldier marched out of the city. But the "Battle of Little Rock" continued.

In July, at the NAACP convention, Mrs. Bates and the "Little Rock Nine" were to receive the Spingarn Medal "for their pioneer role in upholding the basic ideals of American democracy in the face of continuing harassment and constant threats of bodily injury." Together, they flew to Cleveland, Ohio, to receive the award before a wildly applauding audience. However, when Mrs. Bates returned to the city she had once had such faith in, another burning cross was outside the window—the symbol of death. And in September, 1958, the governor decreed that the schools in Little Rock—for both Negro and white—would remain closed indefinitely. Private schools were opened for most of the whites; but the Negro community was without public education.

Nowhere in the deep South was there any further attempt to carry out the Supreme Court decision. The people waited to see what was going to happen in Little Rock.

Slowly, forces to reopen the schools gathered together from among the heretofore silent white citizens. The group banding together in 1959 did not declare themselves for integration, although it was known that if the schools opened at all, Negro children would have to be admitted. A new school board was elected whose members had declared themselves in favor of reopening the schools. Yet, their first act was to dismiss Virgil Blossom as superintendent. Little Rock citizens, it seemed, could not forgive him for trying, even in a small way, to uphold the law of the land.

By the summer of 1959, the law by which Governor Faubus had ordered the schools closed was declared unconstitutional. Again, Negro American children who wanted to transfer to the white high schools were ordered to register.

When Mrs. Bates heard the news, she was in New York to attend the Fiftieth Anniversary Convention of the NAACP and to receive another of the national honors that had been bestowed upon her and the valiant students. She hurried home and, once more, reporters and photographers from all over the world crowded into her home to watch the integration of Little Rock schools. Once more, the authorities began screening the applicants, thirty-three in number, whittling the number down this time to seven. Only two of the original nine would go back to Central High. Jefferson Thomas and Carlotta Walls still had a year of high school left. The rest had been tutored during the year of the closed schools, and were either ready for college or had scholarships for schools in New York or California. Three of the new applicants would be accepted at Tech High and two at the new high school on the west side of town—accepted, that is, unless they could be forced to withdraw of their own accord.

Withdraw? The word brought back a bad memory. A memory almost two years old.

One morning, in the fall of 1957, about a week before the schools were to open, a well-dressed white woman, a stranger, had rung the Bates doorbell.

"I represent a group of Christian women," she had announced. "I have come, Mrs. Bates, to appeal to you as a Southern woman."

"Won't you come in?" Daisy Bates, recalling the scene, felt her pulse racing as it had that day. Her irrepressible hopes had soared. Maybe peace *would* come between white and black in Little Rock!

The woman's next words dispelled all hope. "We want you to use your influence to get the Negro students to withdraw their applications and go back to the colored schools where they belong." She recommended a press conference announcing that Mrs. Bates no longer supported Negro children in their venture. "Advise them to give up." she said abruptly. "Of course, you'll be criticised by the Northern agitators, but don't let them worry you. Southern Christian women will stand by you."

"You've told me what would happen if I withdraw my support from the students. What would happen if I didn't?"

"You'll be destroyed. You, your newspaper, your reputation." The woman looked around the pretty room with cold, appraising eyes. "Everything."

Daisy Bates had been silent. She knew, even then, that this woman was capable of carrying out her threat. For two years, advertising, which means the difference between life and death on a newspaper, had gone down, down, until they were just able to meet expenses. If they missed one payment on their press, the bank would call their loan.

Her visitor rose to leave. "This is my telephone number." She held out a penciled card. "You have until nine o'clock tomorrow morning to give us your answer."

Left alone, Mrs. Bates had started out to the back yard, where her husband was working in the press building. She could hear the buzz, buzz of the turning press. Tomorrow was publication day. She knew that she ought to talk over the matter with her husband. Sixteen years of his life were involved. And he was no longer young. If the *State Press* died, he'd never get another paper. And for these last years, he had stood at her side like a ramrod.

But if she let the children down . . . "If I back down now," she had said to herself, "all the sacrifice will go for nothing. All America is waiting to see what Little Rock will do. Thurgood Marshall said that Little Rock was the key."

Over and over through the night, her mind turned this way and that. There had been only one answer. "In the struggle for freedom there can be no compromise, no turning back."

Not until after she had phoned the woman the next morning to tell her they were going ahead, despite the warnings, did she tell her husband what she had done.

The graying man listened intently. Tears had come to

his eyes. "You did the right thing, Daisy." That was all he said that autumn day in 1957.

But this was 1959.

Two years! That's all the time it had taken the Southern Christian white women to carry out their promise.

"You'll be destroyed," the messenger had said, "You, your newspaper, your reputation."

Daisy Bates wandered over to the newspaper office. She looked at her husband's desk, piled up with papers, at the clippings fastened to the wall, at the beautiful press that never would be paid for. The accountant had made it clear that the *State Press* could no longer carry on. Its assets would have to be sold to pay the debts that had piled up in the last two years of advertising famine. That's how the White Citizens' Council had managed it: by intimidation, slander, and economic power, they had succeeded in destroying the paper that had meant almost as much to her as it did to her husband.

And sooner than even she realized, on October 29, 1959 at 5 p.m., the *State Press* would be dead.

But to take away their livelihood was *all* the White Citizens Council could do, she realized. It had happened to white friends, too. Reverend Ogden had been forced to resign from his church because he walked with the children. Mr. Ashmore had lost his job as editor of the *Gazette*. And the same thing had happened to many others. Yet their reputations had not suffered because they did right. Neither were they destroyed. They had kept on fighting, as her husband would. Knowing what was going to happen to the paper eventually, he had already agreed to become Field Secretary for the NAACP.

"It's only if I let myself hate that I can be destroyed," Daisy Bates said to herself. Her foster-father's words had come to her so often in these last years. Suppose she had backed down? A printing press was only a piece of machinery. Its loss was a small price to pay for the right of seven children—and the seven times seven who would follow after—to be able to walk this morning into an unsegregated schoolroom, not as Negroes, not as non-Negroes, but as *people* with rights and purposes.

Daisy Bates had not done the job alone, of course. But occasionally, for a time or place or particular circumstance, it is given a person to be indispensable. In Little Rock, Arkansas, at the moment of the 1954 decision, a Daisy Bates was necessary. And, as Thurgood Marshall had said, "Little Rock was the key."

7 / When Freedom Is a Cup of Coffee

Storms and shadows thicken
Here is fairing weather
Negro and a white man
Picketing together!

KENNETH PORTER / *Street Scene—1946*

Spring comes early in the South. The spring of 1960 was no exception; but over the February landscape there hung an air of hesitancy. The redbud trees swelled with un-opened blossoms, the jonquils seemed slow to unfurl, and over the Negro communities there hung a silence of wait-ing. The hard-bought victories of Montgomery and Little Rock suddenly seemed small when measured against the giant of injustice still stalking the land.

The working people of Montgomery, who had shown the other Negroes of the South that they did have power when they acted together, now sat where they liked when they rode the buses. But they had made no further protest against other forms of discrimination.

Thirty Negro children out of waiting thousands attended white schools in Little Rock. But Daisy Bates and her husband, with hundreds of other Arkansas Negroes, were still paying the cost of that battle.

Four years had gone by since Martin Luther King, Jr. had forged the weapon of non-violent mass protest. The Southern Christian Leadership Conference he had established had eighty-five affiliated groups working in the deep South and supported with money raised by Negro churches in the East, the Midwest, and beyond the Rockies. The SCLC had busy headquarters in Atlanta, Georgia. But they had not been able to silence the segregationists' shouts of "Never."

The spark so boldly lit seemed, to many, to be flickering out.

But W. E. B. Du Bois, then a very old man, observed "No sound effort is in vain, least of all a struggle with a high ideal." And the Negro Liberation Movement had for its ideal the Declaration of Independence itself, and believed that in non-violent mass action they had a means of carrying out its ideal. The sparks of Montgomery and Little Rock were merely smoldering, not dead. Like a forest fire gone underground that bursts forth suddenly in an unexpected place, so the freedom movement came suddenly alive in the hushed expectancy just before springtime.

In Greensboro, North Carolina, on the first day of February, four students in an all-Negro college walked down the street from their campus to Woolworth's to buy some school supplies. They were waited on. Across the aisle was the lunch counter. But the counter where coffee and food was served did not welcome Negroes. Instead, an all too familiar sign hung above the counter: *We reserve the right to refuse service, etc.*

The Greensboro Woolworth's was a branch of a great chain of stores stretching up and down and across the nation. Everywhere, except in the Southern states, the lunch counters were open to all customers. Only in the South did the management enforce discrimination against the Negro people. The managers called the policy "conforming to local laws and customs."

Joseph McNeill, one of the four students, had the day before tried to get a bite to eat and a cup of coffee at the lunch counter of the local bus station. He had been refused service and the rude refusal had hurt. Trudging back to the college, he had asked himself bitterly, "What's the use of an education without freedom?" And freedom, at that moment, meant simply the right to buy a cup of coffee.

Being turned away from the lunch counter was only one of the daily humiliations McNeill had been subjected to all his life. This time it stirred him to a plan of resistance. The visit to Woolworth's with his friends was the first step in his program.

The four walked over and sat down at the counter. They were indignantly refused service. But, instead of leaving, the four continued to sit and sit and sit until policemen had to come to arrest them, "for disturbing the peace." They were taken to jail and, next day, ten students sat at Woolworth's counter. On the following day, a hundred were marching on a picket line. The "sit-ins" had begun!

The local head of the NAACP, Dr. George Simpkins, was called on for advice and assistance. The legal defense lawyers of the NAACP promised to defend the young students, and Martin Luther King, Jr., through the Southern Christian Leadership Conference, arranged to give financial support. But in Greensboro, Dr. Simpkins realized that the students who had acted so spontaneously needed training. He turned to a small civil rights organization that had not been accustomed to taking action in the South.

The Congress of Racial Equality (CORE) had been founded in Chicago in 1942 by a group of Negro and white friends who were moved by Mahatma Ghandi's non-violent campaign for freedom in India. They had decided that non-violent action, on a small scale, could be useful in opening restaurants and theatres to Negro customers in Chicago and in other cities of the North. The method they had used ever since 1942 was similar to the spontaneous sit-ins of the Greensboro students. But the teams of Negroes and whites belonging to CORE had successfully protested *customs* of segregation in Northern cities. They had not been confronted with local Southern Jim Crow *laws*.

In 1957, a small CORE chapter had helped place Negro children in the first grade of a white school in Nashville, Tennessee. The head of the Greensboro NAACP undoubtably knew of this activity. He may also have heard of the committee for voter registration a CORE worker in South Carolina had started. In any case, at Dr. Simpkins' request, Gordon Carey and James Peck of the staff in the national CORE office (now situated in New York) hurried down to Greensboro to set up a training class in non-violent protest techniques. They were joined by Len Holt, a Negro civil rights lawyer. With Dr. King's warm support and the benefit of CORE's long experience, the Greensboro students staged a six-month-long struggle before they won. And before it was over, hundreds of black students—and some whites from a nearby college—went to jail. This was non-violent mass action every young person in the South could respond to.

Five hundred miles farther south, the spark flared up. The students of Alabama State College in Montgomery had not had a part in the bus boycott of their elders, but they had not forgotten it. For them, too, a cup of coffee became a symbol of the freedoms they longed for and did not have. They marched to the capitol building to the lunch counter on publicly-owned property and sat, unserved, until they, too, were taken off to jail.

"The clock jumped and history changed." Student non-violent action against Jim Crow laws swept the Southern states. Sit-ins; kneel-ins for the right to worship; read-ins at segregated public libraries; wade-ins on the wide expanse of Southern beaches—everything was tried. Southern students, white and black together, walked picket lines singing and carrying signs explaining their purpose. They sat, hour after hour, at lunch counters. They were hooted at by white mobs, beaten, and jailed. But nothing tempted them to retaliate against their tormentors.

Going to jail became a badge of honor. One young Negro student from prison wrote to his mother, "Try to understand, Mama, that what I am doing is right. It isn't like going to jail for a crime like stealing. It is for the betterment of America."

Within a few months, one hundred and thirty-four communities had opened heretofore segregated facilities to Negro Americans. James Farmer, a charter member of CORE, watched the jails filling up, listened to the freedom songs growing louder, and wrote, "The greatest progress will not be made in Congress or the Supreme Court but in the jails."

James Farmer

In February, 1960, a large, dark man in overalls sat on a stump near a campfire in the wide, open Tennessee field that had become, in the last year, the tent-city of Haywood County. James Farmer was forty-one years old, over six feet tall, and weighed two hundred and ten pounds. Sitting there listening to the singing, joining in now and then, he could easily have been taken for one of the displaced sharecroppers who had been driven from their homes on nearby plantations for the crime of registering to vote. But Farmer, though the grandson of a Georgia slave, had never farmed in his life. He was a scholar—had been a labor organizer, a leader in the civil rights struggle, a founder of CORE, and at the moment was serving as National Program Director for the NAACP. When the situation rose in Haywood County, he had come as a representative of the NAACP to see what could be done for these American "refugees."

Except for the lawyers of the NAACP Legal Defense and Education Fund, the national officers rarely played an active role in the South. As Program Director, in charge of this—among many—NAACP problem, James Farmer had intended, months ago, merely to make a flying trip to the area. However, except for one or two flights back to New York on business for the NAACP and to be with his wife and two-year-old daughter, he had already stayed in Haywood County for almost a year. The right of these people to vote was being argued through the courts. The displaced farmers now had shelter of a sort—in tents supplied by a committee of interested people. They had food. But food and shelter were not the only problem. The people were isolated, cut off from American society—even from their own segregated society of Tennessee—by eviction for daring to register to vote. Farmers without land, men and women without a future, singing in the twilight.

James Farmer had started the weekly sings to give the group a feeling of solidarity among themselves and because he loved the old Southern freedom songs. And he worked with and through an *ad hoc* committee directing, suggesting, requesting, and distributing carloads of food, clothes, and tents. Eventually he helped set up a craft re-training program, and many of the Haywood Negroes made leather bags which were sold to raise funds. It was Farmer who worked on setting up a whole new community through which these people managed to survive.

Farmer had been born in Texas, educated there until he came, at the age of 18, to take graduate work at Howard University Divinity School. Nevertheless, Jim Farmer no longer thought of the South as home, any more than he thought of himself as a Negro fighting for his place in the sun. He was a human being remaking a world so that human beings could live together in freedom. For eighteen years now, he had worked closely with whites for the things that they both believed in. His first job when he came to

Chicago had been with The Fellowship of Reconciliation, a pacifist group almost all Caucasian. They were gentle, humanitarian people devoted to the Christian concept of brotherhood and to the spread of the doctrine of non-violent action then being practiced by Mahatma Ghandi.

It was while Farmer was working as Race Relations Secretary at the Fellowship office that he had written a pamphlet showing how Ghandi's non-violent philosophy might be a suitable weapon for American Negroes. A friend had read the article before it was typed up. Impressed by it, he showed Farmer's pamphlet to a few other young people. (They were all young then. Farmer, himself, was barely twenty-two.) That's how the Congress of Racial Equality—CORE—started.

"Funny how things work out," Farmer said to himself that evening by the fire in the tent-city of Haywood County. "For eighteen years we used non-violent means of action for desegregating public places and never thought of mass action in the South!"

Now the earth was shaking all over the South with the victories won against Jim Crow laws by the very same ideas. "And those sit-in kids are bucking Jim Crow *laws*, not just custom as we did when we went into that first restaurant outside of Chicago—a Negro couple and a white team following, asking to be served." Farmer admitted to himself, "Of course, Dr. King has gone into the philosophy a lot deeper than I did, and he puts it to the people with smashing eloquence." Farmer felt a sense of pride in the role CORE had been able to play in sending down trained whites and Negroes from the North to help.

The one thing Farmer had insisted on from the beginning in 1942, was that discrimination and prejudice of one race for members of another affected *all* of America, just as breaking down the prejudice freed everybody. CORE's quiet, patient negotiations; then, if negotiation and persuasion failed, the disciplined action of picketing, sitting-in, giving kind words back for insults, had turned opponents into friends. He had seen it happen again and again. CORE members had been *willing* to suffer for what they believed to be right, but had rarely met with physical attack—never anything similar to what was going on today.

Farmer knew the conditions in the South first-hand, and the reports he had received of the violence and the jailings had not surprised him. He had spent two years in the 1940's trying to organize interracial locals of the upholsterer's union in the Southern states.

As the months went by and CORE got deeper and deeper into the struggle, Farmer had begun to wonder what he was doing in Haywood County, almost on the sidelines. The problem of the evictions was not resolved. Farmer felt that the NAACP had been of some help, but he didn't know how the NAACP *could* resolve it. He did know that the Negro student revolution was cracking the Jim Crow system in the South. A system that had *created* the problem of Haywood County!

"It's all tangled together," he said to himself. "The NAACP school fight seemed to be the final answer when I went into the national office five years ago. Then came the Montgomery bus boycott, out of which has grown King's Southern Christian Leadership Conference and now, the student movement and CORE. But, what's my role in all this? Where do I belong?"

In his overall pocket, he carried a letter from his wife. Ever since they were married in 1949, in New York, Lulu Farmer had worked for CORE. She had stored the records in her bureau drawer when CORE had no regular office of its own. Before Farmer left for Tennessee, the organization had rented a small office, on Park Row, in New York, "no bigger than a telephone booth" as Jim Peck, the tireless young Eastern worker, had said. Now, Lulu had written, the expanding CORE office was almost unrecognizeable. Four paid staff workers. Endless volunteers busy with mailings. Peck and Jim Robinson answering calls from distant places where new branches were being started, or calls for bail from field workers in southern jails. And there was a big national convention coming up, with delegates from all over the country.

He pulled the letter out, unfolded it, and leaned closer to the light-giving flames. He wanted to read Lulu's last sentence again: *"They need you, Jim. Can't you come home?"*

Farmer got to New York on the first day of February, 1961; CORE's National Convention was already in progress. The convention hall was jam-packed. Where had all the people come from?

"We've got a hundred branches, Jim," his wife whispered, "represented by delegates and alternates. And then there's the press and radio and TV."

Farmer's face broke into a big smile. Eighteen years they had plugged away, and hardly anybody had heard of CORE and its non-violent resistance until now!

Sandy-haired Jim Peck was on the platform, calling for reports from the Southern students. Peck was not a charter member of CORE. He hadn't come into the movement until 1946, but before that he had spent time in jail for his pacifist convictions. He was intense, dedicated to the CORE philosophy, and with a talent for getting into trouble. He was not only non-violent in action but in his whole attitude. He really had the love for his enemies that Dr. King tried to instill.

"We'll hear from Miss Patricia Stephens," he said.

A pretty young girl from A&M college in Tallahasse, Florida, stood up and told of her jail experience. She had just come from serving a sixty-day sentence: "So here I am with seven other CORE members . . . we plan to carry on the struggle. I feel I shall be ready to go to jail again if necessary."

Another, a boy, from Rock Hill, South Carolina, followed her. He told of having spent time in solitary confinement. For several days, the prison guards had objected to the sit-in students singing hymns during the morning devotions they had initiated. "We were told to cut out that fuss and, of course, we refused," the boy explained. "The prison superintendent came and put us down in solitary, with no pallet to sleep on and bread and water once a day. White and black. Separate but equal in their misery," he chuckled. "Even in solitary there is no togetherness. I had a hard time explaining to my grandmother," he went on, "why I wouldn't let her bail me out. She was still puzzled when I told her that it was a privilege for a Negro to go to jail for his rights."

One after the other, they told their stories of jail, of the attacks by mobs with sticks and baseball bats. Almost everyone spoke of the songs. One of the young speakers quoted Dr. King who had called the freedom songs the "soul of the movement." "They are more," he had said over and over, "than just incantation designed to invigorate a campaign. They are adaptations of the slave songs, as old as American history. We sing freedom songs for the same reason the slaves sang them, for we, too, are in bondage and the songs add hope to our determination that we shall overcome, white and black together. 'We shall overcome someday.' "

James Farmer sat in the crowded hall and listened and dreamed dreams until his wife put her hand on his and squeezed it.

"They want you to speak, Jim," she said.

Afterward, he couldn't remember what he had said, but he must have reached the delegates, because when somebody nominated him right afterward to be CORE's first National Director, the delegates voted him in with a voice vote. The applause after the vote threatened to go on indefinitely. To still the hand clapping, Farmer said, "Let's sing."

They sang "Nobody's Goin' to Turn Me Around" and, all through the song, that audience of more than two hundred kept looking to Jim Farmer as if they expected him to point out "the road to freedom."

James Farmer decided he had to resign from his NAACP job to take on a larger responsibility. Others would handle the Haywood County problems, but to Farmer, the problems were bigger than a single county.

When it came time to discuss future actions, a proposal was made to plan an interracial bus ride through the South to test a recent ruling that all accommodations in interstate travel must be open to every ticket holder without discrimination as to race or color.

Jim Peck told the story of the earlier "Journey of Reconciliation" he and Farmer had taken part in. This ride, sponsored in 1951 by The Fellowship of Reconciliation, had been a successful venture to the *upper* South. As Peck told it, the ride between Washington and Chapel Hill, North Carolina, had been quite an eventful one. There had been threats and arrests and insults not only for the white and Negro riders, but for NAACP members who gave them overnight lodging and for churches that dared open their doors to the FOR members.

Credit for the idea of this new ride to the deep South belonged to Gordon Carey, CORE's field director, and to Thomas Gaither, hero of the Rock Hill sit-in. Its purpose, Peck explained, would be to test conditions in the buses themselves and in waiting rooms and eating places at the stations. The Interstate Commerce Commission had ordered the stations integrated. The law would be on their side. It remained to be seen whether the law was being carried out in the deep South.

The delegates voted enthusiastically to undertake the project. Volunteers were called for. James Farmer was the first to volunteer; Jim Peck was next. Not all were chosen at the convention, but the date was set for May 1, the starting place, Washington, D.C. One thing still had to be decided. Should the ride be called a "Journey of Reconciliation" as before?

"We don't need a lot of long words to describe a freedom ride," Tom Gaither said.

So, the plan for the first Freedom Ride of 1961 came into being. It was up to the new National Director of CORE to carry out the plans. But first he had to go to the NAACP office and offer his resignation.

On the first day of May, 1961, thirteen Freedom Riders met at a Fellowship House in Washington for their final training. A New England professor and his wife, both in their sixties, a minister, college men and women on their summer vacations, several students from the sit-in movement from the South—it was a dedicated little army.

Earlier, Farmer had sent Tom Gaither to map out a route and to arrange stopping places where they could stay overnight and hold meetings. Each stopover had to be in a different state because the law forbidding segregation of eating places and waiting rooms—the law they were testing —applied only to interstate travel. Finding sleeping quarters where Negroes and whites would be equally welcomed had not been easy. Even invitations to private homes were extended at a risk to the hosts.

However, Gaither arrived in Washington with complete schedules of the Trailways and Greyhound Buses. The sixteen Freedom Riders would divide into two groups so as to be able to compare conditions on both bus lines from Virginia to the Carolinas, through Georgia and Alabama and Mississippi to New Orleans. The rides would begin on May 4. With stopovers, the trip would end on May 17th, with a great celebration in New Orleans for the seventh anniversary of the historic Supreme Court decision.

"The thing I like best about this plan is that it will give our people from the North a knowledge of the South," Farmer said as he and Jim Peck watched the Freedom Riders line up to take the two regular buses into the South. "They'll come home realizing that it's all one country and knowing how rough our problems are."

A few days later, the two leaders happened to be riding

on the Greyhound bus together. Everything on the way had been unbelievably peaceful, from northern Virginia to Greensboro, North Carolina. Both groups had met the night before in Greensboro, at a rally presided over by Dr. Simpkins, whose call had brought CORE into the sit-in movement.

"I wanted our Northern friends to come down to learn a thing or two about Southern segregation," Farmer said with a rueful laugh. "I'm the one that's being educated! Unbelievable, the improvement since I was in this area working for the unions!"

But, James Farmer spoke too soon. At the next stop, an arrest took place. Henry Thomas, one of the Negro riders, was refused a shoeshine in the section of the bus station reserved for white passengers. Charged with trespassing, he was led away in handcuffs, rejoining the party a day later, in Rock Hill, South Carolina. Thomas was just in time to see two hoodlums slugging his friend, John Lewis. Lewis, small and slight, put up his hands to protect his head and eyes. Otherwise, he made no move to defend himself. He had been a senior in the American Baptist Seminary in Nashville, Tennessee, when the sit-in movement got under way, and had gone through a year-long campaign sparked by CORE. Calm acceptance of violence was old stuff to him. His companion, Albert Bigelow, a tall, gray-haired naval commander from Boston, took his cue from John Lewis. White and black together took the blows.

But incidents such as these were sandwiched in between the heartening absence of segregation in other South Carolina and Georgia towns. A person might have imagined himself in a bus station in the North or West instead of the deep South, where politicians had vowed that integration would never be accepted.

In Atlanta, the Freedom Riders were welcomed by a large group of students who had participated in sit-ins. The evening was spent with Martin Luther King, Jr. The outward contrast between the two leaders in the nonviolent resistance movement was great. James Farmer was ten years older, a head taller than King. In every way, he seemed more vigorous. Both men were intellectuals, readers, and thinkers, but Farmer was quicker to act. He had the feeling, on that first evening with King, that he was in the presence of a poet and dreamer, a man catapulted into action by the needs of his people.

"Given a different world, a different time," he thought, "Dr. King would choose the realm of ideas. He's a scholar. For myself, I like to be out with people. I guess I'm a natural-born Freedom Rider," he concluded at the end of the evening, with an easygoing, comfortable smile.

But the Freedom Ride—that first one, which was to make history—was over for James Farmer. In the middle of the night, in Atlanta, he received a telegram that his father had died. By dawn, he was in a plane on his way to the little town in Texas, where his father, a freedom-loving scholar like King, had lived out his life in segregated solitude.

It was only when he saw the headlines on the newstands that Jim Farmer knew that the bus—the Greyhound Freedom Bus—he would have been on had been surrounded and burned in Anniston, Alabama by an angry mob. Swollen jaws, burns, smoke-filled lungs, head wounds. The whole miserable story was before his eyes in print. These were his friends! And the Freedom Rides were his responsibility. He was the Executive Director of CORE. Heartsick, he read on, of the other passengers on the bus who *helped* the mob attack, of the hostility of the townsmen when the most seriously injured were taken by ambulances back to Anniston, of the wild rescue ride of the Reverend Fred Shuttlesworth, who had driven sixty miles to bring the other riders to Birmingham. The next edition of the paper brought more of the story. Jim Peck's picture was on the front page in Texas as it was that day in every paper across the country. Peck with blood dripping from a head wound that required fifty-three stitches to close. The assault on Peck and the other riders in the second bus—the Trailways group—had taken place in Birmingham. Was this the end of the Freedom Ride that had started so peacefully? Would the Riders never reach New Orleans?

Jim Farmer wired and phoned and tried to get news. At last, on the morning of the second day, he got a message from New York. Peck was out of the hospital. He and all the Riders had tried to continue to their destination, but no bus would take them. They had finally boarded an airplane and were safe in New Orleans. The first Freedom Ride was ended.

"But not mine," Jim Farmer said grimly. He was determined to take up the ride where he had left it and go through to the end.

A second Freedom Ride took only a short time to arrange. There was no lack of volunteers. And, there was John Lewis, who had left the first Ride at Sumter, South Carolina to go back to Nashville to take his final examinations at the seminary. Like Farmer, John Lewis wanted to finish his Ride. Between them, they chose and trained ten volunteers, and set off from Nashville.

Just before the bus closed its doors, Henry Thomas hopped aboard.

"But you finished your ride," James Farmer said, looking at an unhealed scar on the boy's head.

"Freedom Rides get to be a habit, I guess," Thomas answered. "Anyway testing bus stations stopped at Birmingham. You can't see what's going on in a bus station in Montgomery or in Jackson, Mississippi from an airplane!"

The police in Birmingham had advance notice of the second Freedom Ride. When the bus from Nashville rolled in, the Freedom Riders were taken from the bus by officers of the law. Two students—one Negro, one white —were jailed on charges of disturbing the peace and resisting an officer. The two, sitting together in the front of the bus, had refused to move when ordered to do so by a policeman who had come aboard just outside the city. The other eleven were also jailed "in protective custody." James Farmer was not sorry for this. He had been told that a mob of Ku Klux Klansmen was waiting outside the bus station.

After a night in the segregated jail, one of the young girls—a white student from Nashville—left with her father, who had flown down to take her home. The other Riders were herded into a police car by order of Police Commissioner Bull Connor and driven north to the Tennessee state line.

More determined than ever to finish the Freedom Ride, James Farmer and his companions waited eighteen hours before they finally managed to board a Trailways bus headed for Montgomery.

"Where Rosa Parks' 'No' started us off," Diane Nash said.

She and John Lewis had been Nashville high school students in 1955—and they had been marching or sitting or riding for freedom ever since! On the bus, they were joined by several more students, two from New York.

In Montgomery, their next destination, there were no policemen in sight. Instead, a mob blocked the sidewalk outside the station, armed with baseball bats. There was scarcely one of the Riders who was not beaten before the police came up with tear gas to disperse the screaming, hate-filled crowd. Not one of the CORE group raised a hand to defend themselves. As soon as they could make their way through the streets, the Negro leaders of Montgomery—the Reverend Seay, Reverend Abernathy, and other veterans of the year of the boycott—came in cars to bring the battered travelers to the comparative safety of a large Baptist church.

The Reverend Fred Shuttlesworth was on his way from Birmingham to help. Martin Luther King, Jr. heard news of the riot in Chicago and caught a plane into Montgomery. He slipped into a side door of the church through a gathering crowd of rough-looking whites. Inside, a huge crowd of Negro people were listening to the Riders' stories.

Outside, several hundred federal marshals, rushed in by the Attorney General, held back the hoodlums. Cars were being overturned and burned; sirens sounded and above the sirens, the shouted threats of bombing. No one dared leave the church. Through the night, the speaking went on between prayers and song.

When morning came, Montgomery was under martial law. Soldiers and federal marshals walked through the streets with eight hundred armed Alabama troopers under federal command. The federal government asked for and received a court order forbidding Klansmen and other groups and individuals from interfering "with peaceable interstate travel."

Two days later, the Freedom Riders were on a bus, being escorted by federalized Alabama troopers to the Mississippi border, where a Mississippi patrol took over. The number of Freedom Riders had now grown to twenty-seven. Two rabbis from Chicago, several Eastern college professors, and more Nashville and Montgomery students, white and Negro, had thrown in their lot with James Farmer and the others.

In Montgomery, as the bus had rolled away, a shot, fired into old Dr. Seay's car, had shattered his wrist. Before the day was out, three other Negro ministers were under arrest "for disturbing the peace." They were Abernathy, Shuttlesworth, and Wyatt Walker, King's assistant in the Southern Christian Leadership Conference. Over the whole United States, hundreds of thousands of people followed the news of the Freedom Riders' bus as it rolled into Jackson, Mississippi.

To James Farmer, the Jackson bus station resembled a beleaguered fortress. Its gates were lined with police who took the Riders off, one by one, to jail. That segregation of interstate travelers had been illegal for years made no difference to Mississippi judges. James Farmer and the rest of the Freedom Riders were sentenced to sixty days in prison and $200 fines. The college professors and a few others paid their fines, received suspended sentences, and went home to their jobs. On May 29, Farmer and eighteen of those on the second Freedom Ride began to serve their prison terms. For Diane Nash, John Lewis, and a few others, being in jail was no novelty. For James Farmer, the Mississippi jail was his first.

"Jail, at best, is neither a romantic nor a pleasant place," he wrote from the Hinds County cell. "Mississippi jails are no exception . . . but Freedom Riders were definitely a new experience for Mississippi jails. For the first time, the penal authorities in the citadel of segregation had a glimpse of the *New Negro* and the *Emancipated White*. I do not think they can ever be quite the same again after this experience.

"Nor will the other prisoners," he continued, "black or white, be the same again, after seeing, in the flesh, men and women who do not believe segregation to be in the very nature of things, and who are willing to defy it."

From one cell block to the other, girls and men sang old folk songs and gospel songs with new words put to the tunes, telling of the Freedom Ride and its purpose. It was not all singing, however, in the crowded cells. Punishments were severe, the food wretched and, during the forty days Farmer stayed in jail, he worried about the unfulfilled responsibilities waiting for him in the CORE office. He had little news of the outside world except from other prisoners, but he guessed, from the way the jail filled up, that Freedom Rides were starting up over the whole of the United States and that CORE was co-ordinating them. However, until the moment came when, in order to file an appeal, he had to consent to be released on bail, Farmer had no idea of the extent of the movement.

The New York office was bedlam. Instead of one hundred branches, there were now one hundred and fifty. In the North, the members picketed and marched in support of the continued Southern sit-ins. Northern CORE members held sit-ins of their own for equal job opportunities and the right of Negro Americans to buy homes in desirable neighborhoods. And they raised money. In the summer of 1961, CORE alone raised and spent over $200,000 on sit-ins and Freedom Riders. The Southern Christian Leadership Conference had spent as much, and the NAACP National Defense and Education Fund had covered the cost of the appeals to the higher courts.

It seemed to Farmer that every branch wanted him to make a speech in its town. It was an opportunity and a challenge. But to Farmer, the Freedom Rides were the most important need that summer. By bus, by train, by air the number of Riders mounted. Negro ministers and Jewish rabbis rode South and went to jail together. White professors became students, learning from fearless southern Negro youths the art of enduring insult and pain and deprivation. Not only Negro and white, but North and South became unified in the struggle.

By the end of the year, 1600 Riders had spent time in southern jails. The courts were clogged with appeals.

1961 remained the year of the Freedom Rides. The Interstate Commerce Commission issued a ruling that all buses in interstate travel had to display a sign stating: *Seating aboard this vehicle is without regard to race, color, creed, or national origin.* Drivers were required to report any interference with these regulations. Terminal facilities had to be open to all without discrimination.

To James Farmer, this order was the Freedom Riders' vindication.

What Freedom Rides meant to *local* Negro Americans in Mississippi is shown by the fact that Freedom School teachers, voter registration workers, and all the incoming Freedom Fighters, are still affectionately and generally called "Freedom Riders" or just "Riders."

The work of CORE, the work of James Farmer, did not stop with the Freedom Rides. All of the organizations in the Negro Liberation Movement are close knit and depend upon one another; but each makes a special contribution. Under Farmer's influence, the many-sidedness and nation-wide activity of CORE has become especially significant. Without scattering his energies, he has a way of being on every battlefront. Through the Freedom Rides, he has made the people of the United States really aware, for the first time, of what is going on in the deep South.

8 / The Man With the Bulletproof Soul

Blurred
by distance and the haze
of many thousand smokes
the city—born of this mountain—lies
gangling over its ridges and valleys,
a tired child-city, full of aches
and growing pains, unsure of its
powerful nature.

JOHN BEECHER / *Vulcan and Mars Over Birmingham*

For Southern Negroes still in the long shadow cast by slave history, the churches had come to stand as refuges of freedom. In the deep South, as the hundredth year since Emancipation unfolded, almost half of the dark-skinned Americans—about seven of the eighteen million—lived where the leftover myths of white superiority and Negro inferiority had the force of law. Whether in the country places or in the industrial cities, segregation laws continued to pile up. When one was, after long litigation, declared unconstitutional by the Supreme Court, segregationists in local legislatures immediately passed a couple more. The barrier between white and Negro citizens was a wall too high to climb.

On the Negro side of the Jim Crow wall, the churches remained, as they had during the whole dark time since Reconstruction, the center of community life. The great masses of people had no other meeting place. For leadership, they turned to their pastors. From many pulpits, they heard "brotherhood" tied in (as it had been since the Negro churches were founded) with the promise of human equality in the United States Constitution. But action designed to turn their hopes into reality seemed as remote as it had at the beginning of the twentieth century.

For a period, the NAACP brought members of the different congregations together. But, after the 1954 decision by the Supreme Court, the white ruler-class blamed the NAACP lawyers for starting the lawsuits up in Washington. In 1955, the NAACP was outlawed in several Southern states. Alabama was the first. Between 1955 and 1964, no branch of the NAACP could meet in any Alabama city. The segregationists hoped that this ban would safely end the struggle of the Negro people for their constitutional rights. And yet, it was in Montgomery, Alabama that the bus boycott took place—under the leadership of the Negro churches. And sixty miles away, in Birmingham, a young Baptist minister kept raising himself up like a lightning rod, daring the lightning to strike.

Birmingham, a city of over 350,000 inhabitants, is built in a valley and up the surrounding hills. It came into existance after the institution of slavery had been destroyed. The myths and traditions of a slave society proclaimed so loudly by the whites of Birmingham were rooted neither in its soil nor in its history. The climate and the red earth of the hills was not good for growing cotton or any other produce that would have made slave labor profitable. It is estimated that less than a hundred Negro Americans were brought to the Birmingham valley as slaves before the Civil War. Yet, today, more than a third of the population is Negro. They came in to help lay tracks for the railroad lines; to dig coal and iron ore and to shovel the coal into the maws of the blast furnaces; to pour the molten iron and haul away the waste to the slag piles. They came to make steel. Birmingham is a city built on steel.

A huge, clumsily-fashioned statue of Vulcan, the Roman god of metalwork, stands as a symbol of Birmingham. The statue is prized by its citizens but, since the spring of 1963, the city has, for many, a new symbol. He is a thin, wiry Negro minister with scars on his back and arms: the Reverend Frederick Shuttlesworth, the "man with the bulletproof soul."

Fred Shuttlesworth

Tall, spare, loose-jointed, exuberant, the Reverend Fred Shuttlesworth walks the streets of Birmingham as though he had not a care in the world. There is laughter in his deep-set eyes when he recounts his running battle with the city authorities. Bombings, beatings, and the Birmingham jails have left him undaunted. It is only when he considers pain and injustice visited on the thousands of his fellow citizens, that the twisted smile leaves his lips and his eyes darken with pain.

When asked, not long ago, how many years he had been fighting segregation, he laughed. "Ever since I was born. Certainly, ever since I can remember anything, I've been committed."

Commitment is a word that comes up often in his talk with the young people he has gathered around him. "Total commitment to the cause of human rights," he tells them, "doesn't leave any room in your body or your soul for hate or fear."

Shuttlesworth was born in Birmingham in 1922 into an atmosphere of violence born of the determination after World War I of the great majority of the white people in Alabama to "keep the Negro in his place." The economic depression of his boyhood days gave way slowly to still more violence when labor unions were trying to get a foothold in the steel mills. To the repressions of the regular police were added the "company cops." This was when Bull Connor entered the picture—as a guard in the steel mills—when Fred Shuttlesworth was only a boy in his early teens. "Bull" was only a name to Shuttlesworth, a fable. It was not until Shuttlesworth came back from theological school that Connor had become a power in the city government.

Fred Shuttlesworth took over the ministry of the small Sixteenth Avenue Baptist Church in a city divided not only between white and black, but divided within the Negro community. There were no Negro police, none in any civil service jobs. There were a few well-to-do Negro lawyers and doctors and businessmen, who for the most part kept aloof from the great mass of workers. The majority of Birmingham's Negro population worked in the blast furnaces and mills, or as porters in the stores, or went to the fancy white homes in the hills to work as butlers, chauffeurs, and cooks. On Sunday, each Negro congregation kept to itself.

The Birmingham Negroes were a people cowed, brutally intimidated, and doing nothing—or almost nothing—about it. Except for the few years when the union had carried on its struggle, the only organization in the whole city that attempted to break down the wall of segregation or that raised even a timid voice against the Jim Crow laws was a small branch of the NAACP. It had been founded as early as 1920, two years before Fred Shuttlesworth was born. Constant harassment and a sort of hopelessness had kept its membership small, its influence meager. By 1950, the Birmingham branch of the NAACP had all it could do just to stay alive.

When the Supreme Court decree was issued in 1954 for desegregating schools, white agitation against the NAACP redoubled. It became the segregationists' whipping boy. A year later, the sound of marching feet in the Montgomery bus boycott was the last straw. Laws were hurriedly passed, demanding that the officers of the local branch of the NAACP reveal the names of the members. This they refused to do, knowing that every person on the membership list would have been out of a job. The Birmingham branch was forced to disband. The organization was outlawed by this simple method everywhere in Alabama.

Birmingham Negroes were left without even this small voice to speak for freedom.

"They can outlaw an *organization*, but they can't outlaw the *movement* of a people determined to be free," Fred Shuttlesworth declared.

He had been spending a good deal of time in Montgomery and had seen how the venerable Reverend Seay, Ralph Abernathy, Ed Nixon, and the youthful Martin Luther King, Jr. had been able to unify the Negro community around the churches.

Almost immediately, Shuttlesworth took action. He brought together a committee of four other Birmingham ministers, a woman of tremendous energy in church work, a lawyer, and a few businessmen who agreed that something ought to be done about Birmingham. With Bull Connor now on the city council and serving as police commissioner, Negroes in Birmingham were victims of a reign of terror. Three of the ministers joined Fred Shuttlesworth in a call for a mass meeting at his church on the evening of June 6, 1956. They doubted whether people would dare to come, but they were willing to give his idea a try.

The night before, the four men sat up late working out a name and a declaration of principles. The name Fred Shuttlesworth suggested, the *Alabama Christian Movement for Human Rights* was long and cumbersome. But to him, every word was important—*Alabama* had to stay in because the people in every community in the state were suffering from the same discriminations. *Christian* couldn't be left out because the church was, for all of them, the center of community life. But the struggle encompassed something even broader than Christian brotherhood.

There was the concept of democracy to be considered, and the longing for liberty that is in every man.

"That's why I think our movement should stand for *Human Rights.*" he said. "Human rights takes in everybody." His eyes twinkled in amusement. "I'd make Bull Connor welcome, if he ever came to his senses."

Shuttlesworth's proposed Declaration of Principles had no catchy slogans. He was asking the people to join in a long, hard crusade that challenged the whole structure of the society under which they were forced to live. He wanted the people to understand clearly the task to which they would be committing themselves. The Governor had said, "If they (the Negroes) keep this up, they are going to find what they're looking for—trouble. Somebody will be getting killed."

Trouble was what these black Americans already had. What they were looking for was justice. And if somebody had to get killed, Fred Shuttlesworth was willing that it be himself.

The church on Monday, June 6, 1956, was as full as it could get. When the men and women had crowded every pew, latecomers stood in the back and along the walls. The founding committee, now a dozen strong, sat in chairs in back of the pulpit. On the lectern, next to the Bible, lay a copy of the Principles, written out in Mrs. Shuttlesworth's clear script. After an opening prayer and a hymn, Fred Shuttlesworth stepped forward to read the declaration and move for its adoption.

A. *As free and independent citizens of the United States of America, and the State of Alabama, we express pub-*

licly our determination to press forward persistently for freedom and democracy, and the removal from our society of any form of second class citizenship.

"To press forward—that means action!" Shuttlesworth banged the lectern for emphasis.

B. *We are not echoing the sentiments of outsiders; but our own convictions and will to be free, so help us God. We will not become rabble rousers; but will be sober, firm, patient, and resolute, within the framework of good will.*

The young minister paused in his reading to explain that their hands were outstretched to those other citizens of Birmingham, the ones on the other side of the Jim Crow wall. He thought it a tragedy that there was no communication between white and black.

Fred Shuttlesworth continued reading to a silent and intent audience. A statement on the enforcement of decrees of the federal court; another on "states rights," declaring that the first right of a state is to guarantee each of its citizens the *same* rights and privileges. Section E called on the city officials to enforce the rulings of the federal court that public facilities in interstate travel and the schools be open to all. There followed praise for the non-violent struggle being conducted in Montgomery. Then Shuttlesworth read the seventh section of the long document:

G. *As to "gradualism," we hold that it means to move forward slowly, maybe, but surely. . . . We want a beginning now! We have already waited one hundred years!*

One hundred years! The people shook the walls with their "amens." Fred Shuttlesworth had to raise his hand for quiet before he could read the final passage.

H. *We Negroes shall never become enemies of the white people. We are all Americans; but America was born in the struggle for freedom from tyranny and oppression. We shall never bomb any homes or lynch any person; but we must, because of history and the future, march to complete freedom—with unbowed heads, praying hearts, and an unyielding determination. . . .*

The Declaration of Principles was adopted. The Reverend Fred Shuttlesworth was elected president of the new organization, the first in Birmingham to unite the body of Negro people into one brotherhood for freedom. The final action of the meeting before adjournment was to name every Monday night meeting night in one of the churches.

No white newspaper printed the Declaration of Principles. No white ministers read it in their churches. The whites just kept repeating that Birmingham Negroes were satisfied with things as they were.

For eight years, the Negroes of Birmingham had come together on Monday nights "to pray, to plan, to prod." A few months after the founding of the Alabama Christian Movement for Human Rights in Birmingham, the Southern Christian Leadership Conference brought together similar groups pledged to help each other. Martin Luther King, Jr. was made president, Fred Shuttlesworth, secretary, of the SCLC. Within a few years, affiliation with SCLC was to have a momentous effect on the history of Birmingham. Almost at once, it served to make Shuttlesworth a nationally known figure, called to speak before huge audiences from New York to California. He was loved for his wit, his courage, his commitment to the cause of humanity, but above all, for the enemies he had made at home.

For so many years in Birmingham, it had been taken for granted that the Negro was on the bottom, the white man on the top. The mayor-police commissioner, Eugene "Bull" Connor, took care that nothing should be changed. "Police brutality was an unquestioned and unchallenged reality," Dr. King wrote of conditions in Alabama's largest city in 1963. " 'Bull' Connor prided himself on knowing how to handle the Negro. . . . He displayed as much contempt for the rights of the Negro as he did defiance of the authority of the federal government."

Bull Connor did not act alone. He had the full support of the city and state governments. In his double capacity of mayor and police commissioner, it could be said that he *was* the government! If he needed any new laws to enforce his authority, he had only to request them, and they were put on the books. Rough, violent, insensitive, he had blocked not only progress toward a democratic way of life for Birmingham Negroes, but also every avenue through which they had been able to appeal to the more moderate and well-meaning whites for twenty years.

Birmingham Negroes could not vote against this man in elections, because scarcely one-tenth of the group had managed to register to vote. They could not go to public meetings to register their complaints. There was a law against interracial meetings. They could not go privately to the homes of any white people they might happen to know. Small groups had been arrested and jailed for meeting in a private home to discuss injustices. Bull Connor had established a rule of fear, a police state.

This was the kind of man Fred Shuttlesworth appeared before, just one week after the June 6 mass meeting. In the name of the Alabama Christian Movement for Human Rights, he respectfully requested of Police Commissioner Connor and his colleagues that Negroes be hired on the police force. The refusal was blunt and final.

But Shuttlesworth was not a man to give up easily. He followed the first request with further petitions and delegations. When these attempts at negotiations failed, he filed a lawsuit demanding the right of Negroes to take examinations as other citizens could for all civil service jobs. Under court ruling, the city had to allow Negroes to take the examination. None were hired. A new lawsuit had to be prepared. Though Shuttlesworth did not win this skirmish, the action marked the wiry, dark-skinned minister as Public Enemy No. 1 in Bull Connor's eyes.

Shuttlesworth consolidated that position by his next move. In line with the ruling against segregated city buses, he asked the city officials to desegregate Birmingham's buses. They refused. The Alabama Christian Movement for Human Rights announced that on the day after Christmas, its representatives would ride in the front seats of the buses.

On Christmas Eve, the Reverend Shuttlesworth's house was bombed and a wall of his church badly damaged. (This was the first of more than twenty unpunished and "unsolved" bombings of homes and churches of Birmingham's Negroes.)

On December 26, as promised, Shuttlesworth led a large

group downtown to board the buses. He and twenty-six other riders were thrown into jail. When they had paid their fines and were released, Shuttlesworth promptly filed suit to desegregate Birmingham buses. The long road through the courts began. Funds raised in the North for the SCLC were used co-operatively by the eighty-five affiliate organizations, of which Shuttlesworth's Alabama Human Rights Committee was one. Delay followed delay. In spite of the federal decree, the black people in Birmingham were compelled to ride in the back seats. In January, 1958 the members of the Alabama Christian Movement for Human Rights decided that they would stay off the buses for awhile, as the Montgomery people had done.

Bull Connor decreed that no Negro minister could tell his congregation to stay off the buses!

"Only God can tell me what to say in my pulpit," Fred Shuttlesworth answered. "I'm going to tell my people to stay off those buses if I have to go to Kilby prison."

Meanwhile, in September, 1957, the same week that the Little Rock children were confronted with armed soldiers to keep them out of their school, Reverend and Mrs. Shuttlesworth with one other minister, took four students, including Shuttlesworth's own two daughters, to the Phillips High School (for whites) to enroll them. They were turned away at the door. At the bottom of the flight of stone steps, a hastily gathered crowd of whites was waiting. Mrs. Shuttlesworth was stabbed, one of the children was hurt, and Fred Shuttlesworth was brutally beaten with chains. Bull Connor's police stood by while ambulances took them off to the hospital. Undaunted, Shuttlesworth filed a lawsuit. Seven more years went by before compliance was won. His daughters had long since graduated from the "separate and unequal" schools reserved for Negroes.

Each move of the people in their valiant resistance against second class citizenship was met with threats and intimidation and frequent loss of jobs. Shuttlesworth's car was confiscated by the state during a libel suit brought by state officials. His driver's license was suspended without cause, and he was jailed about once a month on trumped-up charges. And every jailing meant not only fines but brutal beatings. Still, the people met every Monday night, to pray, to plan, to prod. Every night volunteers stood guard in front of Shuttlesworth's house. The police arrested them. Others took their places.

Through Fred Shuttlesworth, the Negro community in Birmingham became part of the nationwide freedom movement. They did not begrudge the sacrifice.

In 1960, when the students of the small Negro college in Birmingham staged a sit-in, Shuttlesworth joined their picket lines. He suffered the usual arrest, accompanied by a beating in jail.

Then came the Freedom Rides, and the burning of the bus on the road outside Anniston. The uninjured Riders were beleaguered soldiers in enemy territory. And it was to Fred Shuttlesworth they turned for help.

Shuttlesworth did not hesitate. He was sixty miles away with no car of his own, when three cars were offered for the journey. The Freedom Riders were picked up, and then they started back to the Shuttlesworth home.

But there was additional trouble. The second bus load of Freedom Riders was due to arrive at the Greyhound station and Shuttlesworth knew that a mob of Ku Klux

Klanners was gathering. If only he could be in two places at once!

The attack at the bus station was reported on the car radio as he turned into his driveway. Then the broadcaster's voice stopped abruptly. Another voice came on to say that the newsman had been dragged from his car.

The Riders sat numb with anxiety in the Shuttlesworth living room while Mrs. Shuttlesworth twirled the dials, but no further news came through. Her husband paced the floor.

At last, the victims of the assault began arriving in taxis. Since Shuttlesworth was their Birmingham representative, they naturally rallied at his house. Blood dripped from Jim Peck's head wounds. Shuttlesworth helped him into the house.

"You need to go to a hospital," he said and put in a call for an ambulance. "For a white patient," he added. No "white" could be driven in a "colored" ambulance, no "black" in a "white" ambulance. That was the law. It was also the law that no white person could visit in the home of a Negro, but the Shuttlesworths risked arrest to offer their home as headquarters for the Freedom Riders.

Eight hours later, Jim Peck called from the hospital that he was ready to leave. Fred Shuttlesworth went himself to fetch Peck to his home. The car was followed by police on the return trip. A white and a Negro in a car together—that, too, was against the Birmingham law!

Getting the Riders out of the city presented new problems. The Riders wanted to continue their bus trip, but no bus would take them. They decided to try for an airplane flight direct to New Orleans, their final destination. In cars supplied by the members of the Human

Rights organization, they rode to the airport. The mob was on hand but, by this time, Bull Connor had had enough notoriety, and his police kept order. The first two planes, fearing trouble, canceled their flights. At ten that night, Fred Shuttlesworth finally saw the Riders safe on a plane. On the way back to his house, he was arrested and taken to jail.

After the Freedom Rides, the bus companies decided to comply with the year-old desegregation order. The "white" and "colored" signs came down in the Birmingham bus stations.

But the tensions had begun to wear down Mrs. Shuttlesworth's health. The children were also under constant harassment. When an offer came to Reverend Shuttlesworth to become pastor of a large church in Cincinnati, Ohio, he decided to accept, with the proviso that every Monday, and at whatever other times the Movement needed him, he would fly back to Birmingham. The Cincinnati congregation was pleased with the arrangement for, in this way, they could help the Movement in the South.

It was a strange world Fred Shuttlesworth lived in during the summer of 1962. His congregation in Cincinnati saw him only on weekends. But his family was safe in the comparative peacefulness of an Ohio city. Weekdays, Shuttlesworth spent in and out of the Birmingham jail.

"What can you do," Shuttlesworth kept wondering, "about a police commissioner who doesn't know how to rule by law, but only by fear?"

He and Martin Luther King discussed the problem every time they were together. The fear, King commented, was felt not only by the black oppressed but also in the hearts of the white oppressors. Guilt was part of their fear, as well as the dread of change. They had forgotten (or had never learned) to think of their fellow citizens simply as ordinary people, with whom one lived and worked and went to school. Change, to them, was the terrible threat of being punished for what they were doing to dark-skinned individuals. The whites had the idea that, if they weren't on top, then they would naturally be on the bottom.

It was the same in other parts of the South. "Certainly," King wrote several years later, "Birmingham had its white moderates who disapproved of Bull Connor's tactics. Certainly Birmingham had its decent white citizens who privately deplored the maltreatment of Negroes. But they remained publicly silent. It was a silence born of fear— fear of social, political, and economic reprisals. The ultimate tragedy of Birmingham was not the brutality of the bad people, but the silence of the good people."

This was the conclusion Martin Luther King and Fred Shuttlesworth came to in 1962. But the problem was— what could be done about it?

"I won't give up unless they kill me," Shuttlesworth said slowly. "You know, you have to be willing to die before you can begin to live."

In May 1962, Dr. King's group had considered joining the Alabama Christian Movement for Human Rights in a massive campaign against every form of segregation in Birmingham. The Southern Christian Leadership Conference had been formed for the purpose of mutual help. The demonstration of unity, he said, could take place in September when delegates from all the eighty-five affiliated groups would come to Birmingham for their annual convention. What better place to make a stand than in the "most segregated city in the South?"

The rumor of the September campaign came to the ears of some of the older, more moderate, white business men in Birmingham. Perhaps leaving everything in the hands of Bull Connor was not the best way, they said to one another. A group calling itself the "Committee of Senior Citizens" let it be known that they would be willing to meet with the president of the Negro college, with a few of the well-to-do Negro citizens, even with Reverend Shuttlesworth whom they hated the most, if necessary, to negotiate the removal of Jim Crow signs in some of the stores before the SCLC conference and to work out changes in the local segregation laws.

Fred Shuttlesworth was encouraged, though he was not sure that any agreement would be carried out. He called a press conference and announced that the Alabama Christian Movement for Human Rights would, for the time being, conduct no mass demonstrations. The Southern Christian Leadership Conference would hold its convention as planned. After the convention, he said, if the agreements were not carried through, the leaders of SCLC would be asked to return to help launch an action campaign against Birmingham's unconstitutional segregation laws.

As promised, some Jim Crow signs came down. The convention met. The delegates, the reporters, and the cameramen from the metropolitan papers went back to their homes. Then, the signs at the drinking fountains, at the lunch counters in the stores, the insulting signs of segregation, went up again. The segregation laws stayed on the books.

King and Shuttlesworth agreed that no other course was open to them except to move ahead with a direct-action campaign, a campaign supported by the full weight of SCLC affiliates and all the other civil rights movement groups. This was especially necessary since the federal government had let it be known that the passage through Congress of the promised nation-wide Civil Rights Bill was being postponed. There were so many other problems to deal with, the Negroes would have to wait.

"We can't ask our people to wait any longer," Shuttlesworth said quietly.

Plans to begin the campaign several weeks before Easter in March 1963, were made with the greatest care and secrecy. The campaign would center around a refusal to spend money for Easter clothing in stores that discriminated against Negroes. However, protest against every form of segregation would be emphasized. The Easter boycott in Birmingham would be accompanied by marches and mass meetings and prayer.

But there developed a delicate problem of timing. A city election was to take place on March 5. For the first time in years, the white moderates were supporting two candidates in opposition to Eugene Bull Connor. If Connor were defeated, it might be possible to conduct a more peaceful, fruitful demonstration.

Shuttlesworth suggested that the opening of the campaign be postponed until after the election. And so it was. The election was held and, as last minute plans were again underway for the Easter boycott, the returns came in. No candidate for Mayor had received a majority of the votes! A "run-off" election between Bull Connor and Albert Boutwell, the two candidates with the most votes, would have to be held. The non-violent campaign was postponed again. The new date decided upon was not made public. However, King and Shuttlesworth agreed privately that the first demonstrations would begin the day after the run-off election.

In the run-off, much to everyone's surprise, Connor was defeated by the white voters of the city! The news augured well, even though Boutwell had made no claims to be in favor of an integrated Birmingham.

The moment of optimism was cut short, however, when Connor and other city commissioners refused to move out of the City Hall that night. The matter would have to be decided in court and could not be ruled on until after Easter!

"It's unfortunate," Shuttlesworth said, "but I don't see anything to do but to go ahead with our program." King agreed wholeheartedly.

At a huge mass meeting, the plan was unfolded. Doubts on the timing were quieted. The crusade against segregation in the country's most segregated city would begin with Connor still holding the reigns of power.

For three days, sit-ins by students were held at lunch counters in the downtown stores. Thirty-five young men and women were arrested and went quietly to jail. (They went, knowing that the SCLC had arranged in advance to have on hand a large sum for bail money. They would be free again in five days.) On Saturday, several hundred Birmingham citizens from the Negro community marched to City Hall to announce the opening of the boycott. The march was led by Fred Shuttlesworth, who never asked anyone to go where he was not willing to lead.

The sidewalks on the line of march were jammed with cheering Negroes. The stores had no Negro customers— the Easter finery they would have bought stayed on the store shelves. Sit-ins in the public library, kneel-ins in the segregated churches, crowds at the court house waiting in line to register to vote! A non-violent army without weapons was on the march. There were hundreds of arrests. The jail filled up and the cash for bail was dwindling. Bull Connor was everywhere directing the arrests, but strangely, he had restrained himself from his usual violence.

Then a familiar blow was struck. The city government obtained a court order forbidding any further activity until the right to demonstrate had been argued through the courts. Similar orders had halted protests in other states. By court order, the NAACP branches in the South had been destroyed. Court orders could delay the liberation movement everywhere. The right to assemble, the right to protest peacefully, was clearly guaranteed by the Constitution, and had been upheld repeatedly, but everytime a suit was brought, legal appeals through state courts and up to the United States Supreme Court moved at a snail's pace.

Martin Luther King announced to the papers, "We are not lawless people, but we believe that the courts of Alabama have misused the judicial process to perpetuate injustice. We cannot, in good conscience, obey."

Two days later, on Good Friday, for the first time since the movement began, the Negroes in Birmingham marched in disobedience of a court order. Fifty chosen people, with Martin Luther King and Ralph Abernathy in the lead, marched from Zion Hill Church toward the City Hall. All fifty were arrested and hauled off to jail.

Shuttlesworth was not on this march. He had another pressing responsibility. The carefully laid plans for financing bail bonds after the cash funds were spent had fallen through. Yet money must be found if King and Abernathy and several hundred others were to be released to appeal.

It was an anxious eight days, both for the leaders in prison and for Shuttlesworth and the others outside. But people all over the United States understood that the Birmingham campaign must not be allowed to fail. Birmingham Negroes brought to Shuttlesworth such sums as they could spare. Even children came, bringing their dimes and quarters. But it was a phone call from Harry Belafonte, the singer and actor, in New York that relieved the tension. He had collected all the funds needed. The jail doors opened. King and Abernathy and their comrades in prison were freed.

"I've been thinking," Dr. King said to Fred Shuttlesworth and his entire staff. "Two-thirds of the people who have submitted to arrest have been adults. It's time now to involve the young people. The boys and girls in the high schools understand that they have a stake in freedom and justice."

"They're ready," Shuttlesworth answered confidently. He knew; he had always kept in close touch with the young people in the community even though he was, now technically, a minister in Cincinnati.

On the first day that the children were allowed to march, more than a thousand went, singing, off to jail.

The jails filled up and still they came, one day, two days. On the third day of the children's march, Bull Con-

nor cast off all reserve. Police dogs and fire hoses to break up the demonstrations were held in readiness.

Connor gave the order, "Dammit, turn on the hoses."

The marchers, adult and children, did not fight back against the dogs or the violent streams of water. But neither did they turn back. Shuttlesworth was beaten to the sidewalk from the pounding force of the stream of water turned on him. As he was being taken on a stretcher to an ambulance, Bull Connor was heard to say, "I wish he'd been carried away in a hearse."

"In the face of this resolution and bravery," Dr. King wrote afterward, "the moral conscience of the nation was deeply stirred, and all over the country our fight became the fight of decent people, Americans everywhere, of all races and creeds."

President Kennedy sent down Burke Marshall, a lawyer in the department of justice, to mediate. He sent no troops to intervene, but he let it be known that he had them nearby, in reserve.

Things happened quickly after that. Committees were appointed to negotiate. Separate committees at first, because the white citizens would not meet face to face with Negro leaders. However, in the end, even that would come to pass. While the negotiations were going forward, thousands of Negroes stood daily in the downtown streets, singing freedom songs.

On Friday, May 10, an agreement was announced. Public facilities in the downtown stores would be opened to *all* customers; Negroes would be hired for jobs previously denied them; all persons still in jail would be released; and (most important of all) a pledge was given to open, within two weeks, direct communication between whites and Negroes to discuss problems of mutual concern. It might be thought that these were small gains for so much suffering. The Negroes of Birmingham did not think so. Nor, apparently did Bull Connor's followers.

The agreement set off new violence in the part of the city where the Negro population lived. The home of Dr. King's brother was bombed that night, and another bomb was exploded in the room of the Gaston Motel where Shuttlesworth, King, and the other leaders had been in the habit of conferring. Several people were hurt. The bombs started a Negro riot, and soon the Negro section of town was sealed off. It was a night of terror. But the agreement held.

On May 23, by order of the highest Alabama court, Eugene Connor gave up all claim to his power. The more moderate elected officers took over.

It was a moment of quiet thankfulness for Fred Shuttlesworth. "The walls that were to preserve segregation now, segregation tomorrow, and segregation forever, are falling flat," he said at the Monday mass meeting. "Birmingham is practically desegregated by law. We must work more diligently now so that Birmingham may be integrated. Integration is the order of the day."

Before the month was out, President John F. Kennedy sent a message to the Congress urging immediate consideration of the Civil Rights Bill. People all over the country prepared to march in Washington, as an affirmation of their determination to see the legislation enacted.

"Our judgment of Bull Connor should not be too harsh," President Kennedy said. "After all, in his way, he has done a good deal for civil rights legislation this year."

Nevertheless, there came a shadow over that period of national confidence in final victory. And the shadow was cast once again from Birmingham, Alabama. On Sunday, September 1963, a bomb exploded in the Sixteenth Avenue Baptist Church just across the street from the Human Rights Headquarters. The church was the one Fred Shuttlesworth had presided over for so long, the one to which he still returned every Monday night, the church from which he had led the eager children who marched for their freedom. When the explosion occurred, Sunday School was in session. Four young girls, Cynthia Wesely, Denise McNair, Carol Robertson, and Addie Mac Collins were killed. Two other young Negroes, Johnny Robinson and Virgil Wade, were fatally shot during the disturbances that followed the bombing. The death of these six children was a bitter end to the high hopes of midsummer.

The assassination of John F. Kennedy came only a month later as the pressure for passage of strong civil rights legislation mounted in the Congress. Nine months later, Lyndon B. Johnson signed the Civil Rights Bill of 1964.

All over the South, plans had been made to test compliance with the provisions of the bill, especially those completely forbidding discrimination in all places open to the public. Acceptance of desegregation over the South was by no means complete, but in Birmingham, Alabama, the same young boys and girls of high school age who had withstood the snarling dogs and the fire hoses, who had gone to jail for freedom, now went out from the Alabama Christian Movement for Human Rights headquarters to eat in "white" restaurants, to go to the "white" moving picture theatres. On that July day, no one was refused admittance, no one was insulted.

In spite of the fact that an interracial council had been set up as promised, no whites in Birmingham thought of joining the testing that day. Whites and Negroes in Birmingham still did not know one another.

Desegregation, of a sort, had come to the city. *Integration* was a long way off.

And what of Fred Shuttlesworth? Though he has his family home and his pastorate in Cincinnati, Birmingham Negroes still claim him as their own; and not Birmingham alone, but all of Alabama. Shuttlesworth was in Selma in the voter registration drive in the spring of 1965. He was in the forefront of the triumphant fifty-mile march to the capitol building in Montgomery. He has assumed a new and important responsibility as President of the Southern Conference Education Fund, the oldest and most influential integrated group working for human rights in the South.

How long? How hard the route to be traveled? Fred Shuttlesworth hesitates to guess. He keeps on praying and planning and prodding, at whatever risk. His commitment to freedom is total.

"You have to be prepared to die before you can begin to live."

9 / "We Shall Overcome"

"I can't believe that I have
to hate anybody
and when I do,
it will only be out of fear
and I'll know it."

BOB DYLAN / *Poem*

In Raleigh, North Carolina, at Easter time, 1960, when
the history-making sit-ins were beginning to sweep through
the South like a cleansing wind, a conference was called
of the students, Negro and white, who had played an active
role. The Southern Christian Leadership Conference and
the field workers sent down from the North by CORE
had assumed the responsibility for financing and training
the students in the principles and tactics of non-violent
resistance. But CORE had far-flung national interests,

projects initiated by local branches in their own communities. The Southern Christian Leadership Conference was composed of dedicated ministers. However, they were responsible first to their own congregations and to their communities. Although local branches of the NAACP gave limited support to mass action, their traditional mode of protest was through the courts. When Negro leaders made compromises with the white business communities, it was the students who refused to give up their demonstrations. Some of the adults, with their livelihoods to think of, began to speak of caution. Were the students going too fast, too far? Ought not the young people stay in college and finish their education?

Youth from the Southern high schools and colleges wanted to be part of the great campaigns planned in high places; but they also wanted to make their own contribution, at their own pace, in their own way. Education was important to them, but freedom came first.

Martin Luther King, Jr. could sympathize with their impatience. He was young enough himself to remember how it felt with hopes too long deferred. Yet he had doubts about the wisdom of a separate student organization. It was Ella Baker, working at the time in the Atlanta office of the Southern Christian Leadership Conference, who spoke up for the young rebels. In the Raleigh meeting hall, she looked beyond the rows of young men and women, mostly from the South, mostly Negro with a sprinkling of fair-skinned faces, and addressed herself to the adult observers in the rear.

"The younger generation is challenging you and me," she said. "They are asking us to forget our laziness and doubt and fear and to follow our dedication to the truth to the bitter end."

It was agreed, after long discussion, that a temporary committee be set up "to promote communication and coordination" of student protest activities. This temporary committee met with Mrs. Baker and Dr. King many times during the summer. In October, 1960, the Student Non-violent Coordinating Committee was formally organized. At the October meeting, sixteen working staff members were chosen. Jane Stembridge, from Virginia, acted as temporary office secretary until she returned to her studies at Union Theological Seminary in New York. E. B. King, from Kentucky, was chosen as temporary Executive Director. When he resigned to enter law school, James Forman, took his place. Forman was thirty-three years old, a Chicagoan with a degree from Roosevelt College and graduate credits from two Eastern colleges. Charles McDew, a student, like most of the staff from the deep South, was elected chairman. The new organization (spelled SNCC, pronounced *Snick*) was given for headquarters, a "windowless cubicle" in the offices of the Southern Christian Leadership Conference on Auburn Street in Atlanta. Except for a young poet, Julian Bond, in charge of publicity and Bob Moses, a teacher from a private school in New York City, all sixteen members were students who chose to defer college careers for a year or more "to do things their own way, by putting their bodies on the line." Only one of the students was not a Negro. Bob Zellner was a white Alabaman who had been moved to action by the Montgomery bus boycott.

The SNCC workers became the shock troops, the troubleshooters. They were also, in that first tumultuous year, the patient grass-roots pioneers in the fear-ridden rural sections of Georgia, Alabama, and Mississippi. They understood the tedious, tiring, always dangerous job of encouraging local leaders to come forward.

Comedian Dick Gregory, singers Bob Dylan, and Pete Seeger, and Guy Carawan of Highlander Folk School were their troubadours; Ella Baker, their mentor. Funds for their small budget came from Dr. King's group, from the Southern Conference Educational Fund, an old interracial organization based in New Orleans, and from donations raised on Northern campuses by students fired with the realization that they, too, were part of the "challenging generation."

When the Freedom Rides started, SNCC workers were on every bus, had their heads bloodied, and went to jail. Where local sit-ins ran into bad trouble, SNCC workers joined the picket lines and put their experience to the service of oppressed communities. The mere existence of SNCC had a big impact on the country. Before the year was out, the staff had tripled in number. Enough funds had been raised to rent a small dilapidated house in one of the poorer neighborhoods of Atlanta as home base.

The workers got subsistence wages of ten dollars a week—when funds were available. Housing, for the most part, was provided by families in the community. If necessary, SNCC workers went in the fields and chopped cotton to secure money for food and gas for the donated cars needed to take them around the sparsely-settled counties in the rural South.

Gas sometimes comes before food. In 1963, SNCC workers on a voter registration project lived for a whole week on peanut butter sandwiches.

"It was choice of regular meals or gas for our cars," a staff worker explained. "We needed the cars to bring sharecroppers into the county seat to try to register to vote."

In back of each dramatic moment of lining up a dozen —or a hundred—Negro American citizens before the registrar's office lay months of planning. The awareness that this job had to be undertaken, the fundamental importance of the right of suffrage, is not a new concept in the history of struggle for freedom. From the day of Emancipation from slavery, the right to vote has been a battle cry.

In 1910, "enfranchisement of the Negroes in the South" was a major goal of the newly-founded NAACP. It has been the declared purpose of every civil rights group since then.

Since the 1930's, bills to ensure full voting rights have been put again and again before Congress, and some of them have become law. The courts have taken a hand. Since 1957, the Department of Justice has been empowered to enter the field.

Citizenship-training classes to overcome the barrier of stringent education tests were set up at several places by concerned Southerners, black and white. But the schools reach only a few would-be voters. Besides, education alone does not help where registrars are dedicated to white supremacy, and when a man or woman has to risk economic ruin, a bombed home, and possible death as the price of putting his or her name on an application to register more incentive is needed. Yet without the vote, Negroes in the South have small hope for relief from their suffering.

All this the SNCC staff knew very well. Even in the months when they were picketing and riding Freedom Buses and going to prison, they were giving creative thought to a way to help the Negroes recover their right to vote.

Bob Moses, Harvard-trained teacher, whose early life had been spent in New York's Harlem ghetto, had a plan in his mind. Early in 1961, he proposed that SNCC workers go quietly to live in some community to get to know the people, and try to put them in a position to fight for themselves. He didn't know what a SNCC worker could accomplish, but he did know that there was only one way to find out. That one way was to become part of the community and to build the trust of the people in their *own* capacity to help themselves. Moses asked to be assigned to McComb in southern Mississippi to test his plan.

Mississippi was the state with the worst record of repression of the Negro's right to vote. McComb, a small town, lay in the poorest part of the state in midst of cotton fields tilled by wretchedly-housed sharecroppers or tenant farmers. A man had just recently been shot down on the highway there after trying to register to vote. This was the place Moses chose to live in early in 1961. The experiment ended a few months later with beatings and jailings. Both Bob Moses and Bob Zellner, who had joined him, were among those arrested. The Mississippi courts stepped in and issued an injunction against any more demonstrations in McComb. Not until 1964 were there any meetings held there again.

Nevertheless, the experiment proved its point. SNCC workers were looked to for advice and help. Later, when the drive for voter registration was taken up by all the older civil rights groups—and by the federal government itself—the SNCC workers assumed leadership. In 1963, a giant voter registration drive was projected for Mississippi by the Council of Federated Organizations (COFO), an ad hoc committee composed of all the major civil rights organizations. Bob Moses was chosen as project chairman. The dangerous organizing work was carried on by SNCC and CORE workers.

Working closely with Moses was the new chairman of SNCC, John Lewis.

Like Bob Moses, John Lewis is a thinker and dreamer, but above all, he is a David, challenging the Goliath named Jim Crow.

John Lewis

"The future of American Negroes is in the South. Here, 327 years ago, they began to enter what is now the United States of America; here they have made their greatest contribution to American culture . . . here is the fruitful earth under the beauty of the southern sun; and here, if anywhere, is the need of the thinker, the worker, and the dreamer."

The speaker was Dr. William E. B. Du Bois. The occasion, one of the rare meetings where young Negro southerners and young white southerners had come together. The place, Raleigh, North Carolina, 1947.

At that time, John Lewis, the chairman of the Student Non-violent Coordinating Committee, was about to celebrate his seventh birthday. He was one of ten children on an Alabama farm. He had never heard of Dr. Du Bois. No word of any youth conference in a distant state even drifted to his ears. If anybody had told him that the elderly scholar, the great leader of the Negro people, was speaking to boys like himself when he said the South needed "the thinker, the worker, the dreamer," young John would have leaned back his head and laughed. Nobody needed him, unless it was his mother wanting him to mind the baby, or one of his older brothers ordering him to go feed the chickens. Nobody needed a seven-year-old Negro boy who was kind of small for his age. Not in a family that had so many children.

In 1954, when a Supreme Court judge issued a decree that the public schools could no longer discriminate on the basis of color or race, John Lewis' family was living in Nashville, Tennessee, and he was 14 years old. John Lewis heard about the Supreme Court decision the day it was announced. The news of the decree was, in a way, more exciting to his age group than to any other. Students in the segregated senior high schools were too near the end of their education for the change to make a vital difference. The elementary school children knew about discrimination, but the sense of rejection hurt less in school than in other ways—like not being able to go to parks that had a swimming pool or to buy an ice cream soda down-town.

But serious-minded boys and girls in John Lewis' junior high assumed that next term they would be able to enter a desegregated high school to finish their education.

In 1957, when John Lewis was seventeen years old and a junior in the all-Negro high school, Nashville took its first step toward obeying the Supreme Court desegregation order, and that beginning was not in high school at all! The Nashville plan was to begin with the admission of Negro children to the first grade. One six-year-old, Barbara Jean Watson, attended the Hattie Cotton School. Integration for Barbara Jean lasted one day. That night, the school building was completely destroyed by bombs.

At this point, John Lewis and other young Negroes—and the few sympathetic white people in Nashville—might well have given up. But they didn't. A young white woman, Anna Holden, who had worked once with a CORE group in New York; James Lawson, a young Negro who had been admitted to Vanderbilt University where he was studying to become a minister; Diane Nash, just graduated from the high school John Lewis attended; some NAACP leaders; and mothers in a Negro PTA all banded together. They tried to negotiate with the white community. When that failed, they organized mass protest. They insisted that the Nashville schools be opened in accordance with the Supreme Court's decree. And they won! John Lewis and his high school friends learned the meaning of non-violent resistance for the first time. In spite of jeering mobs, they marched, they sang, they printed and distributed leaflets. Nashville became the first city in the South to open its schools without soldiers standing guard.

The group that had carried through so valiantly did not stop there. Two years later, they enlisted high school and college students in a community campaign to open parks and libraries, to get "white" and "colored" signs removed in the stores downtown.

John Lewis, at this time, was enrolled in the American

Baptist Seminary. He was called on to help train a new generation of high school students in the ways of non-violent action and, for almost a year, they met and marched and picketed. The campaign took time and sacrifice. James Lawson was expelled from Vanderbilt University; Diane Nash and John Lewis and some of the others were arrested and went to jail. Anna Holden, because she was white and on their side, was hooted at by the segregationists. But the crusaders had learned to take insults without hating.

Lewis was a junior at the Seminary when the Greensboro sit-ins began. All winter, Nashville students had been holding workshops, picketing, singing freedom songs, and seriously studying the philosophy of non-violence. They already had in back of them the experience of earlier campaigns. They had even held two quiet, unadvertised sit-ins at a drugstore lunch counter. They were ready.

Sit-ins in sympathy with the Greensboro students were organized by Nashville CORE immediately. The participants were largely college students like John Lewis, but high school boys and girls, who had been trained in non-violence, were welcomed.

Then came a crack in the wall that the segregationists had built. A truce was declared. A citizen's committee of whites and Negroes were conferring when Lewis heard about the student conference Dr. King had called for Easter in Raleigh, North Carolina.

"Suppose some of us went to find out what's going on in other places. Wouldn't that be a good idea?"

James Lawson thought the suggestion a good one. He arranged for John Lewis, a couple of students from Fisk, a young white friend from Vanderbilt, and two or three of the Nashville high school students to make the trip to the conference.

The two-day meeting was a high point in John Lewis' life.

"It's not just Nashville and Greensboro that's moving," he said to himself as he sat in the Shaw University Hall and looked around at the delegates from every state in the South. More than a dozen were Caucasian—no better dressed than the Negroes, not trying to run the show, not telling what ought to be done, but *asking*, wanting to learn.

"We're ready to keep on going if it takes five or six years," one of the Greensboro delegates said. "Whatever time it takes. We're going out to eradicate the whole stigma of being called inferior."

John Lewis had just about made up his mind to quit school at the end of the year, enlist full time in the civil rights movement, and give up the idea of going on to a graduate school. Listening to the discussion groups about the importance of voting and jobs and a dozen other things the students proposed to work for, he realized he had at least better go back and get his degree from the Seminary. If you didn't know anything, you couldn't be very useful.

The temporary committee was set up to plan with Mrs. Baker and Dr. King for some months, but John Lewis was sure a permanent committee would come out of the planning and that someday he would be part of it.

It wasn't easy to stick to his resolve to finish college when October came and the Student Non-violent Coordinating Committee became a reality; but he kept at his books.

March 1961, came in with dogwood trees in bloom in the

park. The gnarled old apple tree on the Divinity School campus was budding. Two more months before final exams and then he would be free to go into the movement. John Lewis was glad he had stuck it out. When SNCC asked him for his experience, he could say he had a B.A. degree. He had been offered a scholarship to Fisk. Maybe he ought to go on to graduate work. He filled out an application to enter Fisk University for the fall session.

But freedom's timetable doesn't go by a college schedule. Anna Holden came back from a CORE meeting in New York with news of the first Freedom Ride to start in May. She asked for volunteers. This ride John Lewis just had to go on! His school work was in good shape. There wouldn't be much going on in May, except reviewing for exams. If the Ride took longer, he could leave it for a few days to take the exams.

John Lewis arranged to be absent from the Seminary for the last three weeks and volunteered to be a Freedom Rider. He worked with fierce energy in a neighborhood filling station every afternoon for six weeks to earn his bus fare.

Washington was a wonder to John Lewis. It was the first large city he had ever seen. History come to life! He stared up at the walls of the Supreme Court where the whole modern civil rights struggle had been started with the school segregation decision.

The bus left from Washington and made its way South towards New Orleans.

Lewis left the other Riders at Sumter, South Carolina to go back to Nashville to take his final examinations. He would only be gone for a few days, he said to James Farmer. He was sorry to miss the stop in Atlanta where they would see Dr. King again. And he was sorry not to be on the Freedom Bus when they got to Alabama, his home state. But he'd be back as soon as he could, rejoining the Ride at Montgomery or at Jackson, Mississippi.

The bus burning in Anniston, the fearful beating of the Riders in Birmingham, all happened while Lewis was taking his examinations. As he was answering questions in blue-backed examination books, the newspaper picture of James Peck with blood running down from his face was before his eyes. He made a vow that somehow he would complete the ride, testing the places the others couldn't manage.

James Farmer joined Lewis in Nashville immediately after his father's funeral. Together, they prepared to complete the journey CORE had mapped out. With eleven others, black and white, they set out on May 17, 1961.

On the now-famous Second Freedom Ride, John Lewis faced his first mob. It was at Montgomery, Alabama. The pain of being clubbed with a baseball bat was unimportant compared to the exultation of seeing that, even under extreme provocation, non-violence could be made to work.

"I'm not going to let those people make me hate 'em," Lewis said grimly to himself as the first blow fell. And, all at once, he didn't hate. He didn't have to practice non-violence; he felt no desire to strike back. *Put your body on the line.*

In Jackson, fines and suspended sentences or jail terms awaited the Riders, whose number had been augmented to twenty-seven. Of these, nineteen chose to go to prison. They were the first of hundreds to be jailed in the Mississippi city before the summer was over. The South was beginning to harvest the bitter fruits of segregation.

Their sentence was for sixty-seven days. After the first two weeks, the jail was over-full. Lewis and Farmer and several other Freedom Riders were moved to Parchman Penitentiary. They were treated badly, but staunchly followed their training in non-violent resistance.

"Is it doing any good?" John Lewis asked a Negro trusty in Parchman. "Outside, I mean."

He could see for himself the change that had come over the long-term Negro prisoners. There was puzzlement, at first, when they heard black and white inmates singing freedom songs back and forth to each other from segregated cells. Then, there was a slow, hesitant show of little kindnesses to the civil rights group. Finally, there were questions that indicated understanding. What John Lewis wanted to know from the trusty was whether the Jackson people were being inspired by the Freedom Rides to resist segregation themselves.

"Well, I'll tell you something I heard happened in Jackson last week." The trusty had gotten the point. "We've got a zoo here—nice green lawns, trees. Benches every so often in front of the animal cages where white folks can sit to watch the bears and lions and monkeys. Naturally, no benches for colored. The other day, a couple of our people sat down on a bench and got themselves arrested. Word got around and four or five more sat down to rest their feet."

"They got arrested, too?" John Lewis was concerned. Mississippi jails were not pleasant places.

"Sure." The trusty chuckled. "The zoo boss started to order some benches for colored. You know, 'separate but equal.' But in light of the fuss you Riders kicked up, that didn't seem a good idea. So, he pulled out *all* the benches. Cut 'em up for firewood. Now they tell that no humans can sit down at the zoo, white *or* colored—only the animals!"

It was late in the summer before James Farmer and John Lewis finally completed their Freedom Ride at the Trailways Station in New Orleans. Farmer was taking a plane to the New York office of CORE. Lewis went with him to the airport.

"You're heading for Fisk this fall, I suppose," Jim Farmer asked.

John Lewis shook his head. "I'm not sure. I'm going to the SNCC headquarters to see if they can use me. You know how it's been talking with people in jail—even the so-called criminals. Every Negro I've talked to wants to do something to improve his miserable condition. Like, for instance, 'taking that walk to the ballot box' Dr. King talks about. But you told me yourself they can't do it alone."

James Farmer nodded. "You're right. But we're behind the times, you and I. While we were taking our little vacation, Bob Moses went down to McComb, and got SNCC's first voter registration project started. CORE intends to do the same kind of thing in Louisiana. That's what I'm rushing back to New York about. If you're going to be working for SNCC, I'll see you around."

It was not the first time Lewis had heard the name of Bob Moses. The Atlanta students in Parchman Penitentiary never got tired of talking about him and trying to explain his ideas. The thirty-one-year-old mathematics teacher from New York had been on the staff in Atlanta ever since

SNCC took permanent form in October 1960. Moses had degrees from two Eastern colleges—Haverford and Harvard —and had been teaching in a good private school until he heard about the Easter meeting in Raleigh. He had resigned his job immediately to come down South.

The next time Farmer and Lewis met, fifteen months had gone by. There was a conference of leaders of the five organizations most active in the Negro Liberation movement. They were going to coordinate plans for the year ahead. Roy Wilkins for the NAACP, Whitney Young for the National Urban League, Martin Luther King, Jr. for the Southern Christian Leadership Conference, James Farmer for CORE. Representing SNCC was shy, sturdy, twenty-year-old John Lewis, the newly elected chairman.

On his way home from the Freedom Ride, Lewis had stopped in the SNCC headquarters. He had filed an application for field work and had had a long talk with Ella Baker. Her advice was for him to go on with his education. She was convinced that SNCC workers needed every bit they could get.

"Don't worry," she said with one of her rare, reassuring smiles, "we'll call you when we need you."

Enrolled in the graduate school at Fisk University, John Lewis forced himself to concentrate on laying out a course of study with his adviser. He attended seminars; he piled books on his desk. But whenever he looked away from an open page, his thoughts shot to the Freedom Movement.

SNCC workers had gone into Albany, Georgia, after some NAACP youth members had been arrested at a quiet lunch counter sit-in. When the NAACP undertook to appeal their conviction, the Albany city government had repealed the segregation ordinances. Nevertheless, Albany police went on arresting people who tried to eat at the lunch counters. The charges were anything from breaking the peace or trespassing to "contributing to the delinquency of a minor."

No permit would be issued for a peaceful march, so Albany citizens and SNCC workers marched without a permit. Hundreds were thrown into the crowded jail. The *Albany Movement* was under way. What had been a minor protest against segregation was on the way to becoming an important struggle for freedom.

That was the moment the call came from SNCC. John Lewis closed his philosophy books, went to Albany, Georgia, and dug in for the duration. He joined James Forman and other civil rights workers in the Albany jail.

Thanksgiving, Christmas, the New Year of 1962—there were high points and low points in the Albany campaign, but never a victory.

It was at Albany that John Lewis made his calm, steady power of endurance count. When the SNCC chairman, Charles McDew, fell sick and resigned, Lewis was elected to the national chairmanship. His concept of the job of a chairman is one who is on the front line of every struggle. Lewis does most of his thinking in jail cells. He "votes for freedom" not only with his feet but with his whole, scarred young body.

A real beginning was made in the Mississippi Voter Registration Project in 1963. Work had begun in more than half of Mississippi's eighty-two counties. Dressed in blue overalls, SNCC and CORE field workers went from door to door and talked with the people. They met thousands of men and women ready to take the risk of trying to regis-

ter. Less than a dozen that first winter succeeded in getting
their names on the books. The laws and regulations, the
bias of registrars, the whole power of the white community
was against them. But they never spoke of turning back.

SCLC continued to furnish financial and moral support.
Local NAACP branches joined in, and a joint committee
calling itself the Council of Federated Organizations
(COFO) was set up under Bob Moses' direction.

In 1964, John Lewis spent as much spare time as he
could working in Mississippi, not to lead but to learn and
to listen, to help find a way to wrench from the state power
structure what people deserved as human beings. But necessary as it was that they have the right to vote, the fact that
1964 was a presidential election year brought up another
serious question. What people needed if they were to be
effective, was to take part in party politics. Choosing candidates and deciding on policies was done through a political
structure from which Negro Americans—registered or not
—were wholly excluded. Almost all Negroes wanted to
support President Johnson when he ran again. They wanted
to be in the Democratic Party. But in Mississippi, the
Democratic Party was run by rabid segregationists like
Senator James Eastland. No black man or women would
be allowed even at a precinct meeting. There would be no
chance to get real representation at the local or state level,
no chance to have any voice in national policies under these
circumstances.

Long discussions were held. Anyone who had the urge
to speak had his say and, gradually, from the discussions
between Lewis and Moses and James Farmer and many
local people, and with advice from the state chairman of
NAACP, Aaron Henry, a plan evolved. Delegates from

every Congressional District in the state—regularly registered voters—were called together in the state capital. At the end of April, 1964, the Mississippi Freedom Democratic Party came into being. MFDP would be the *democratic* Democratic Party for Mississippi, for no one would be excluded.

The party entered candidates in the state primary which was to be held on June 2. Mrs. Fannie Lou Hamer, Mrs. Victoria Gray, and several others filed for Congress. The candidates, with other delegates, were chosen to go to the regular Democratic convention in August.

The big push was on! A thousand volunteer students from other states over the country came down to work under Moses' direction. They recruited potential voters, they taught in Freedom Schools, they organized Freedom Days when hundreds marched to the court houses to register—and more often than not were carted off to jail on trumped-up charges. Undaunted, the Negroes of Mississippi, the COFO workers, and the volunteers went ahead with election work. John Lewis took his share in the day-to-day struggle, though his duties as National Chairman often took him away.

In the regular Mississippi primaries, no MFDP candidates had been elected, but a mock election had been held at the same time. Negroes had polled more *uncounted* votes for their chosen candidates than were cast by the segregationist "regulars". Plans were made to send the MFDP delegates to the Democratic Convention in Atlantic City to contest the seating of the old-line regulars on the ground that they did not—could not—represent Mississippi Democrats.

The Convention challenge of the seats of the representatives from Mississippi made history. It was the first move by a body of Negro voters to change, at the ballot box, the system under which they were forced to live. Millions of people throughout the country, watching the convention on TV, realized that Negro Americans in Mississippi were on their way to freedom and would never turn back. And the delegates won very real support from the members of the convention floor, so much support that the administration was forced to offer a compromise. Two MFDP delegates—Aaron Henry and one other—would be given seats in the Mississippi delegation. But the "regulars" would keep their seats. The other MFDP delegates would be seated on the convention floor "as honored guests."

The decision whether or not to accept the compromise was a difficult one for the Mississippians to decide. John Lewis and the other SNCC workers were opposed. But it was for the delegates themselves to make the decision. Lewis was jubilant when they voted in caucus that all or none must be seated. To be an "honored guest" meant no voice and, therefore, nothing at all. Their refusal to compromise came as a shock to the convention, and was sharply criticized, but their courage in standing up for their rights brought new sympathy for the cause.

The momentous summer passed, and autumn came. But 350 SNCC workers did not leave. They dug in for the duration, "doing things in their own way, putting their bodies on the line."

Congressional candidates of the Mississippi Freedom Democratic Party were denied a place on the ballot in November. Three of them, Mrs. Fannie Lou Hamer, Mrs.

Victoria Gray, and Mrs. Annie Devine decided to run as independent write-in candidates. On election day, COFO also held a "Freedom Election" where thousands of unregistered Negroes were given an opportunity to express their choice. And their choice was Lyndon Johnson for President, Hubert Humphrey for vice-president, and the three MFDP candidates to represent their districts in Congress. This, in John Lewis' view, was no idle gesture. It gave evidence to the nation that if the Negro people had been allowed to register and vote in 1964, Johnson, not Barry Goldwater, would have carried the state. It also laid the basis for the challenge to unseat the Mississippi Congressmen which, in January, 1965, won the votes of 149 members of the House of Representatives!

The success of the Mississippi challenge was evidence to John Lewis of the soundness of the SNCC philosophy. SNCC had tried, from the beginning, to show the isolated Southern Negroes that they held in themselves the power to act. All SNCC had to offer them was encouragement and a method.

It is true, as the leadership of MFDP claims, that without the young students, MFDP might not have come into being. It is equally true that the young workers have learned much from the people among whom they lived! Their goal had not been to become leaders but rather to make themselves *dispensable*. When the people were ready to carry on alone, SNCC would move to another community. They did not desire to be in the limelight—least of all, their young chairman.

A stranger passing John Lewis on the street would see only a short, dark, unassuming young man with a neat

214 I HAVE A DREAM

black mustache and faint scars on his face and scalp. In
fact, only once, in March 1965, did this David of the
Liberation Movement assume giant stature in the sight of
the nation. It was at the climax of two years of struggle
by the Negro people of Selma, Alabama, with the help of
SNCC organizers, to register to vote. There had been,
under the pressure of the sheriff—"a little Bull Connor"—
the usual jailings and beatings. On February 18, a state
trooper shot and killed James Lee Jackson, one of the local
leaders in the Negro Liberation Movement. People outside Selma heard little of this man's death, but Martin
Luther King, Jr. came to Selma to deliver the memorial
for Jackson in the Negro church. Next day, King was arrested and jailed by Sheriff Clarke. The Southern Christian
Leadership Conference determined to bring its enormous
influence to bear on the situation.

A decision had been made to walk in a body to Montgomery, the capital, to petition the governor for redress.
On Sunday, March 7, six hundred men, women, and children gathered in a church in the Negro section of Selma
and walked, four abreast, toward the Montgomery highway. John Lewis was there walking with local leaders at
the front of the line. Martin Luther King had been on
hand working actively during the week, but that Sunday,
he had gone to Atlanta for a conference. He planned to
join the marchers somewhere along the fifty-mile walk.

Just outside the city, where the Montgomery highway
leads over a bridge, state troopers stood, shoulder to shoulder. "You have one minute to disperse!"

The Negroes halted, tense with anxiety. From the front
line, Lewis took one short step forward, a small figure in
a white leather jacket. His hands were in his pockets to

emphasize his posture of non-violence. At his back, the crowd began to kneel for a prayer.

The air was suddenly filled with tear gas. At the same moment, with billy clubs and bull whips, the line of state troopers rushed forward. John Lewis was the first to be struck down. On TV cameras across the nation, Americans saw helmeted soldiers nudge his unconscious figure with their booted toes, as they moved to disperse the terrified crowd. They chased the sobbing, bleeding marchers a mile through town, clubbing them as they ran.

King rushed back to Selma determined to carry through the interrupted march. He called for ministers and others from all over the country to join the people of Selma in exercising their constitutional right of peaceful assembly. The response was overwhelming. Protestants, Jews, and Catholics, clergy and laymen flew into Alabama. Shuttlesworth brought forces from Birmingham, and even a few white Alabamians were moved to join the protest. A new march was quickly planned. It was countered by the governor, who obtained an injunction from the courts forbidding any assemblage on the highway.

Again, state troopers confronted the Albany Negroes and their supporters on the bridge where John Lewis had been struck down.

Dr. King and other notables led this protest march. They bowed to the order of the court, held a minute of prayer, and marched solemnly back through the Selma streets without meeting with violence.

Dr. King drove to Montgomery to plead that the injunction be lifted.

In crowded Selma that evening, white segregationist gangs roamed the streets. Three of the Northern visitors who had come South for the protest were attacked. One of them, James Reeb, a white Unitarian minister from Boston, was fatally beaten. Reeb died two days later in a Birmingham hospital.

All this while, John Lewis lay in the Good Samaritan Hospital with a fractured skull.

On the third day, Lewis insisted on being released from the hospital, though his serious head injury was far from healed. When friends demurred, he released himself. It had been arranged for him to fly North for treatment and rest. But, as chairman of SNCC, John Lewis had no intention of leaving the scene of trouble. He was in for the duration.

Under national pressure and continued demonstrations in Alabama and over the country, Lyndon B. Johnson, on Monday, March 15, delivered an eloquent speech before the two houses of Congress. He promised to use all of his powers to get a new civil rights bill passed which would "strike down restrictions to voting in all elections—federal, state, and local—which have been used to deny Negroes the right to vote." The President also affirmed the marchers in their constitutional right to assemble.

SNCC workers with the Albany leaders listened to the President on the radio. They sat up straight and proud when they heard his eloquent plea that all Americans overcome their intolerance and bigotry. It concluded with the significant words, "We Shall Overcome." The only question was—who did "we" include?

One day after President Johnson's speech, the court injunction against the march was lifted. On the same day, state troopers viciously attacked demonstrators on the grounds of the capital at Montgomery.

From East and West, thousands of concerned men and women poured into Selma. Meetings, marches to the courthouse, memorial services for the murdered minister, James Reeb, occupied every hour. John Lewis slipped unnoticed into the Negro church were the memorial service was held. He sat thinking sorrowfully of the good man who had come so far from his home to meet death. He wondered if Reeb, with so many other Bostonians, had been in the Washington March. The March that had brought so much hope to so many people in the Movement two years ago. John Lewis sighed when he recalled how shocked some people were when he had used that occasion to warn that more, much more, would have to be done by the government before freedom would come.

His thoughts moved to the other James who had also lost his life in the Selma trouble. James Lee Jackson's death had not moved the Selma authorities to relax their violence for a moment. It had caused no stir in the country. James Jackson had a dark skin. James Reeb was fair. Both had given their lives for the same cause. Because of both deaths, Selma would gain a little freedom.

There was a sense of triumph that the victorious march would take place. Elaborate arrangements were going forward. John Lewis had been invited to sit on the platform being erected on the capitol grounds in Montgomery when the march ended. He would walk the fifty miles. But he couldn't help thinking that there could be no victory for

America until the day when the deaths of two men, one black and the other white, were mourned equally by all the people.

John Lewis intended that *that* kind of freedom should not be too distant.

10 / One Day Out of a Long Tomorrow

The truth shall make us free,
The truth shall make us free,
The truth shall make us free, someday,
Deep in my heart, I do believe
We shall overcome someday.

FREEDOM SONG / *We Shall Overcome**

"Where are you going?" a stranger asked a child sitting beside her on a day coach.

"To Washington," the little boy replied, "to get some more freedoms."

All roads led to the national capital that last week of August 1963. From Tallahassee, Florida; Little Rock, Ar-

* *New words and music arr. by Zilphia Horton, Frank Hamilton, Guy Caravan, and Pete Seeger; © Copyright 1960 and 1963 Ludlow Music, Inc., New York, N.Y.; Used by permission.*

kansas; Birmingham, Alabama; Albany, Georgia; Mc-Combs, Mississippi; from New York, Chicago, San Francisco, and Los Angeles, and all the other battle stations, the freedom fighters gathered. By plane, by train, by bus, by bicycle, by scooter, and by foot to bear witness to the great struggle for democracy.

One hundred and eighty-seven years had gone by since the signing of the Declaration of Independence, a hundred since Emancipation, and almost a decade since the Supreme Court decision. The Washington March for Jobs and Freedom had been long in the making. Twenty-two years ago, on the eve of World War II, A. Philip Randolph had proposed a great March of the Negro people as a protest against discrimination in employment. He had succeeded in clearing the way for jobs in defense plants without an actual March; but the usefulness of mass protest had never left his mind. The August 28th March was his idea. To carry it through, he had enlisted the leaders of every organization devoted to Negro liberation. It was to be the largest demonstration for civil rights in history.

The plan, worked out over several months, was to bring masses of people from the organizations, as well as the leaders of the movement, into Washington. Philip Randolph and Bayard Rustin, co-chairmen of the March, hoped to have one hundred thousand people gather together. Their leaders would present certain demands to the government, especially "comprehensive and effective civil rights legislation from the Congress to guarantee *all* Americans the right to vote, access to *all* public accommodations, decent housing, adequate and integrated education, and measures to insure full, equal opportunities of employment."

When the day came, something far beyond the high hopes of Philip Randolph occurred. Instead of a hundred thousand, there converged on Washington almost two hundred and fifty thousand Americans. For this one day, at least, these men, women, and children, from every walk of life, shared the vision of an integrated tomorrow. They looked into each other's eyes, Negro and non-Negro, old and young, and saw the America that *could* be.

We have *desegregation* when the legal bars to racial contact are lifted. This much is indispensable, and was the reason for the urgency in the passage and enforcement of the Civil Rights bill then before Congress.

We have *integration* when contact between individuals is very broad, equal, and unrestricted. The Washington March was integrated. For one day, a mass of Americans walked together, ate together, smiled, and cried together. Together, white and Negro children from every part of the country played happily without any apparent consciousness of skin color. The teen-agers of both races wiggled their bare toes in the cooling waters of the pool in front of the Lincoln Memorial or applauded wildly for their favorite movie stars, white and Negro, who were seated together on the speaker's platform.

Together, gray-haired whites and gray-haired Negroes reminisced about the *other* time, seventeen years ago, when they heard Marian Anderson sing from these same steps. They nodded in solemn agreement when Roy Wilkins interrupted the program to tell of the death in Ghana of William E. B. Du Bois, and to remind the audience that "his was the voice that brought us here today."

"It's like Moses," an old woman cried. "God had written

that he should not enter the Promised Land." Was she white or Negro? The people near her didn't notice. The Washington Marchers were color blind.

Not one ugly incident marred the day; not one voice was raised in hatred. Russell Baker of the *New York Times* commented that "The sweetness and patience of the crowd may have set some sort of national high-water mark in mass decency." And there were none in that huge gathering who appeared willing to accept anything less than a complete overhauling of the way of life that has imprisoned one out of every ten Americans beyond the wall of racial segregation.

The strongest applause came for the most militant speeches. For Fred Shuttlesworth, who opened the program shouting, "Turn the Negro free and America will be free! Freedom! Freedom! Freedom!" For James Farmer's message sent from a Louisiana cell where he had been jailed for picketing a court house in regard to voter registration. For Rabbi Prinz, who had suffered from racial intolerance in a Nazi concentration camp and came to the March with words of warning from his own bitter experience. "The real enemy in the struggle we are waging," he said, "is neither bigotry nor hatred nor intolerance. The real enemy is the indifference of the decent people."

When John Lewis stood up to speak, the crowd gave him an ovation, both because of the hundreds of young crusaders he represented and because they knew that he had been asked to "soften" his speech. But minor revision had not dampened the fire of his words. It was very clear, by the time he finished, that youth—on the platform and in the audience—would be content with nothing less than FREEDOM NOW.

But it was Martin Luther King, Jr., near the close of the afternoon, who gave permanent form to the vision of an integrated tomorrow:

"Even though we face the difficulties of today and tomorrow, I still have a dream," he said. "It is a dream chiefly rooted in the American dream. I have a dream that one day this nation will rise up and live out the true meaning of its creed: 'We hold these truths to be self-evident, that all men are created equal.'

"I have a dream that one day, on the red hills of Georgia, the sons of former slaves and the sons of former slave owners will be able to sit down together at the table of brotherhood.

"I have a dream that one day, even the state of Mississippi, a state sweltering with the heat of injustice, sweltering with the heat of oppression, will be transformed into an oasis of freedom and justice.

"I have a dream that my four little children will one day live in a nation where they will not be judged by the color of their skin, but by the content of their character. This is our hope. This is the faith that I go back to the South with—with this faith, we will be able to hew out of the mountain of despair a stone of hope."

A dream . . . a dream . . . echoes of King's refrain came from the lips of old men and from lively boys swinging on tree limbs above the crowd. It echoed, too, from the part of the platform where six women sat still as statues. Two—Mrs. Medgar Evers and Mrs. Herbert Lee—had seen their husbands killed in the "non-violent" freedom fight. Two others, Mrs. Diane Nash Bevel and Mrs. Gloria Richardson, had jail sentences hanging over their heads. The last two were Mrs. Daisy Bates and Mrs. Rosa Parks.

When the long program was over, when Philip Randolph had spoken the pledge to the future, when the last verses of "We shall overcome" had been sung, the throng seemed reluctant to unlink arms and go home. Were they afraid that when they left the grass and green trees that stretched for a mile between the Lincoln Memorial and the Monument to George Washington, that the dream would desert them? That the integrated, democratic America they longed for was not just around the corner? Did they suddenly remember that thousands in that crowd were going back South to danger, and that John Lewis had pointed out that there was nothing in the proposed Civil Rights Bill "to protect young children and old women from police dogs and fire hoses?"

Was the March an end or a beginning?

James Baldwin said, when the last marchers had gone, "The day was important in itself, and what we do with this day is even more important."

One hundred Negro citizens of Birmingham were part of that gathering in Washington. Two months later, they would be standing before a bombed church in their own city, watching the bodies of four little girls being dug from the rubble.

A bus load of men and women and children would start home for Selma, Alabama when the sun went down. Would this glimpse of a better tomorrow fade before Sheriff Clarke's determined "never"?

Many of the thousands of singing students who marched down Constitution and Independence Avenue would go, after another college term, to teach in Freedom Schools and to help with voter registration. The bodies of two of them, along with a Mississippi-born companion, would be discovered in a common grave outside of Philadelphia, Mississippi.

The hundred and fifty Congressmen who were on the steps of the Lincoln Memorial would corral the votes of enough of their colleagues on Capitol Hill to pass the Civil Rights Bill.

Too soon and too often, Freedom Fighters were called on to make good their pledge of personal sacrifice. Did they realize how long the marching and the singing and the jailings would have to go on? Did their pledge, repeated after Philip Randolph, really mean that those who have had the dream before their eyes would not abandon it?

The eventful months following the Washington March were proof to the leaders of the Negro Liberation Movement that the majority of the American people were casting off their indifference and beginning to grasp the meaning of *Freedom Now*. The response over the country to the tragic bombing in Birmingham, the passage of a strong Civil Rights bill in Congress, the alignment of forces against racism after the nomination of Barry Goldwater for the presidency, the impression made by the delegation of the Mississippi Democratic Freedom Party in Atlantic City, the thousands of volunteers in Mississippi helping with voter registration—all these things seemed good portents.

In October 1964, Martin Luther King was awarded the Nobel Peace Prize for his leadership in the non-violent civil rights movement. His response to the news of this high honor was characteristic.

"I do not consider this merely an honor to me, personally," he said, "but a tribute to the discipline, wise restraint, and majestic courage of the millions of gallant Negroes and white persons of good will who have followed a non-violent course in seeking to establish a reign of justice and a rule of love across this nation of ours." In his acceptance address before the world audience gathered at Oslo, Norway, Dr. King again paid tribute "to the real heroes of the freedom struggle."

"Many of them are young and cultured," he said. "Others are middle-aged and middle class. The majority are poor and untutored. But they are all united in the quiet conviction that it is better to suffer in dignity than to accept segregation in humiliation."

Dr. King went on to name three closely related problems confronting modern man: racial injustice, poverty, and war.

"The struggle to eliminate the evil of racial injustice constitutes one of the major struggles of our time. The present upsurge of the Negro people of the United States grows out of a deep and passionate determination to make freedom and equality a reality 'here' and 'now.' In one sense, the Civil Rights Movement in the United States is a special American phenomenon which must be understood and dealt with in the light of American history. But on another and more important level, what is happening in the United States today is a relatively small part of a world development. . . . What we are seeing now is a freedom explosion, the realization of 'an idea whose time has come'. . . . What the main sections of the Civil Rights movement in the United States are saying is that the demand for dignity, equality, jobs, and citizenship will not be abandoned or diluted or postponed. If that means resistance and conflict, we shall not flinch. We shall not be cowed. We are no longer afraid."

As W. E. B. DuBois, at the opening of the century, restored to young Negro Americans the real image of themselves as worthwhile human beings, so, fifty years later, the eloquence of Martin Luther King, Jr. is restoring words such as Freedom and Democracy to their proper meaning. All America, today, is taking lessons from the spokesmen of the Negro Liberation Movement.

Suggested Reading

This is an approximately chronological reading list intended to enrich and fill in the many gaps in this account of the modern liberation movement. Starred items are particularly suitable for older readers.

BACKGROUND MATERIAL

I / *The African Roots*
 Rogers, J. A.: *Africa's Gift to America*. New York: J. A. Rogers Pub.; 1958.
 Davidson, Basil: *The Lost Cities of Africa*. Boston: Little, Brown and Company; 1959.
 Du Bois, W. E. B.: *The World and Africa*. New York: International Publishers Co.; 1965.

II / *Overall History from 1619 to the Twentieth Century*
 Hughes, Meltzer: *Pictorial History of the Negro in America*. New York: Crown Publishers, Inc.; 1958.

Bontemps, Arna: *Story of the Negro.* New York: Alfred A. Knopf, Inc.; 1948.

*Bennett, Lerone C.: *Before the Mayflower.* Chicago: Johnson Publishing Co.; 1962.

Woodson, Carter: *The Story of the Negro Retold.* Rev. ed. by Charles W. Wesley. Washington, D.C.: Associated Publishers; 1959.

*Aptheker, Herbert: *Essays in the History of the American Negro.* New York: International Publishers Co.; 1963.

*Redding, Saunders: *They Came in Chains.* Philadelphia: J. B. Lippincott Co.; 1950.

III / *Colonial Times to the Middle of the Nineteenth Century*

Graham, Shirley: *Your Most Humble Servant.* New York: Julian Messner, Inc.; 1949.

Yates, Elizabeth: *Amos Fortune, Free Man.* New York: E. P. Dutton & Co., Inc.; 1950.

*Stampp, Kenneth: *The Peculiar Institution.* New York: Alfred A. Knopf, Inc.; 1956.

IV / *The Abolition Movement Through the Civil War*

Du Bois, W. E. B.: *John Brown.* New York: International Publishers Co.; 1962.

Buckmaster, Henrietta: *Flight to Freedom.* New York: Thomas Y. Crowell Company; 1958.

Breyfogle, William: *Make Free.* Philadelphia: J. B. Lippincott Co.; 1958.

Graham, Shirley: *There Was Once A Slave.* New York: Julian Messner, Inc.; 1947.

Douglass, Frederick: *Life and Times of Frederick Douglass.* New York: Collier; 1883.

Sterne, Emma Gelders: *Long Black Schooner.* New York: Scholastic Book Services; 1962.

McCarthy, Agnes and Lawrence Reddick: *Worth Fighting For.* New York: Doubleday & Company, Inc.; 1965.

V / *To the End of the 19th Century*
   *Stampp, Kenneth: *The Era of Reconstruction.* New York: Alfred A. Knopf, Inc.; 1965.
   Washington, Booker T.: *Up From Slavery.* New York: Doubleday & Company, Inc.; 1933.
   Du Bois, W. E. B.: *Souls of Black Folk.* Greenwich: Fawcett; 1901.
   Hughes, Langston and Arna Bontemps: *Poetry of the Negro, 1746–1949.* New York: Doubleday & Company, Inc.; 1949.

THE TWENTIETH CENTURY

I / *Overall*
   Hansberry, Lorraine: *The Movement.* New York: Simon & Schuster, Inc.; 1964.
   *Lomax, Louis: *Negro Revolt.* Harper & Row, Publishers; 1962.
   Hughes, Langston: *The Big Sea.* New York: Hill & Wang, Inc.; 1963.
   Sterne, Emma Gelders: *Mary McLeod Bethune.* New York: Alfred A. Knopf, Inc.; 1957.

II / *The Rising Tide: 1932–1965*
   Anderson, Marian: *My Lord, What A Morning.* New York: The Viking Press; 1956.
   Hughes, Langston: *Fight For Freedom.* New York: W. W. Norton & Company, Inc.; 1962.
   *Braden, Anne: *The Wall Between.* New York: Monthly Review Press; 1958.
   Mulzac, Hugh: *A Star to Steer By.* New York: International Publishers; 1963.
   Gregory, Dick: *Dick Gregory From the Back of the Bus.* New York: E. P. Dutton & Co., Inc.; 1962.
   King, Martin Luther, Jr.: *Stride Toward Freedom.* New York: Harper & Row, Publishers; 1958.

Peck, James: *Freedom Ride*. New York: Simon & Schuster, Inc.; 1962.

Sterling, Dorothy: *Tender Warriors*. New York: Hill & Wang, Inc.; 1958.

Bates, Daisy: *The Long Shadow of Little Rock*. New York: David McKay Co., Inc.; 1962.

Griffin, John Howard: *Black Like Me*. Boston: Houghton Mifflin Company; 1961.

*Smith, Lillian: *Our Faces, Our Words*. New York: W. W. Norton & Company, Inc.; 1964.

King, Martin Luther, Jr.: *Why We Can't Wait*. New York: Harper & Row, Publishers; 1964.

Zinn, Howard: *The New Abolitionists*. Boston: Beacon Press; 1964.

*Baldwin, James: *The Fire Next Time*. New York: The Dial Press, Inc.; 1963.

Index

Index

Index

ABOUT THE AUTHOR

Emma Gelders Sterne is deeply involved in the Civil Rights Movement. Friend and hostess to most of the leaders of the Movement, she has written several books about outstanding Negroes, including MARY MCLEOD BETHUNE and BLOOD BROTHERS. Born in Birmingham, Alabama, and educated at Smith College, Mrs. Sterne has been a teacher and an editor. She now lives in San Jose, California.

Text set in Electra.
Composed at Westcott and Thomson, Philadelphia, Pennsylvania.
Printed by Halliday Litho, West Hanover, Massachusetts.
Bound by Book Press, Brattleboro, Vermont.
Typography by Atha Tehon.